# THE GRADUAL ACCEPTANCE OF THE COPERNICAN THEORY OF THE UNIVERSE

*By*

**DOROTHY STIMSON**

# The Gradual Acceptance Of The Copernican Theory Of The Universe

### *by* Dorothy Stimson

ISBN: 978-93-57487-28-3

**Published by**

## DOUBLE 9 BOOKS

2/13-B, Ansari Road, Daryaganj
New Delhi – 110002
info@double9books.com
www.double9books.com
Tel. 011-40042856

# CONTENTS

# PREFACE

THIS study does not belong in the field of astronomy, but in that of the history of thought; for it is an endeavor to trace the changes in people's beliefs and conceptions in regard to the universe as these were wrought by the dissolution of superstition resulting from the scientific and rationalist movements. The opening chapter is intended to do no more than to review briefly the astronomical theories up to the age of Copernicus, in order to provide a background for the better comprehension of the work of Copernicus and its effects.

Such a study has been rendered possible only by the generous loan of rare books by Professor Herbert D. Foster of Dartmouth College, Professor Edwin E. Slosson of Columbia University, Doctor George A. Plimpton and Major George Haven Putnam, both of New York, and especially by the kindly generosity of Professor David Eugene Smith of Teachers College who placed his unique collection of rare mathematical books at the writer's disposal and gave her many valuable suggestions as to available material. Professors James T. Shotwell and Harold Jacoby of Columbia University have read parts of this study in manuscript. The writer gratefully acknowledges her indebtedness not only to these gentlemen, but to the many others, librarians and their assistants, fellow-students and friends, too numerous to mention individually, whose ready interest and whose suggestions have been of real service, and above all to Professor James Harvey Robinson at whose suggestion and under whose guidance the work was undertaken, and to the Reverend Doctor Henry A. Stimson whose advice and criticism have been an unfailing source of help and encouragement.

# PART ONE AN HISTORICAL SKETCH OF THE HELIOCENTRIC THEORY OF THE UNIVERSE.

## CHAPTER I.
## The Development of Astronomical Thought to 1400 A.D.

### *A Preliminary Sketch of Early Theories as a Background.*

THE appearances in the heavens have from earliest historic ages filled men with wonder and awe; then they gradually became a source of questioning, and thinkers sought for explanations of the daily and nightly phenomena of sun, moon and stars. Scientific astronomy, however, was an impossibility until an exact system of chronology was devised.[1] Meanwhile men puzzled over the shape of the earth, its position in the universe, what the stars were and why the positions of some shifted, and what those fiery comets were that now and again appeared and struck terror to their hearts.

In answer to such questions, the Chaldean thinkers, slightly before the rise of the Greek schools of philosophy, developed the idea of the seven heavens in their crystalline spheres encircling the earth as their center.[2] This conception seems to lie back of both the later Egyptian and Hebraic cosmologies, as well as of the Ptolemaic. Through the visits of Greek philosophers to Egyptian shores this conception helped to shape Greek thought and so indirectly affected western civilization. Thus our heritage in astronomical thought, as in many other lines, comes from the Greeks and the Romans reaching Europe (in part through Arabia and Spain), where it was shaped by the influence of the schools down to the close of the Middle Ages when men began anew to withstand authority in behalf of observation and were not afraid to follow whither their reason led them.

But not all Greek philosophers, it seems,[3] either knew or accepted the Babylonian cosmology.[4] According to Plutarch, though Thales (640?-546? B.C.) and later the Stoics believed the earth to be spherical in form,

Anaximander (610-546? B.C.) thought it to be like a "smooth stony pillar," Anaximenes (6th cent.) like a "table." Beginning with the followers of Thales or perhaps Parmenides (?-500 B.C.), as Diogenes Laërtius claims,[5] a long line of Greek thinkers including Plato (428?-347? B.C.) and Aristotle (384-322 B.C.) placed the earth in the center of the universe. Whether Plato held that the earth "encircled" or "clung" around the axis is a disputed point;[6] but Aristotle claimed it was the fixed and immovable center around which swung the spherical universe with its heaven of fixed stars and its seven concentric circles of the planets kept in their places by their transparent crystalline spheres.[7]

The stars were an even greater problem. Anaximenes thought they were "fastened like nails" in a crystalline firmament, and others thought them to be "fiery plates of gold resembling pictures."[8] But if the heavens were solid, how could the brief presence of a comet be explained?

Among the philosophers were some noted as mathematicians whose leader was Pythagoras (c. 550 B.C.). He and at least one of the members of his school, Eudoxus (409?-356? B.C.), had visited Egypt, according to Diogenes Laërtius,[9] and had in all probability been much interested in and influenced by the astronomical observations made by the Egyptian priests. On the same authority, Pythagoras was the first to declare the earth was round and to discuss the antipodes. He too emphasized the beauty and perfection of the circle and of the sphere in geometry, forms which became fixed for 2000 years as the fittest representations of the perfection of the heavenly bodies.

There was some discussion in Diogenes' time as to the author of the theory of the earth's motion of axial rotation. Diogenes[10] gives the honor to Philolaus (5th cent. B.C.) one of the Pythagoreans, though he adds that others attribute it to Icetas of Syracuse (6th or 5th cent. B.C.). Cicero, however, states[11] the position of Hicetas of Syracuse as a belief in the absolute fixedness of all the heavenly bodies except the earth, which alone moves in the whole universe, and that its rapid revolutions upon its own axis cause the heavens apparently to move and the earth to stand still.

Other thinkers of Syracuse may also have felt the Egyptian influence; for one of the greatest of them, Archimedes (c. 287-212 B.C.), stated the theory of the earth's revolution around the sun as enunciated by Aristarchus of Samos. (Perhaps this is the "hearth-fire of the universe" around which Philolaus imagined the earth to whirl.[12]) In *Arenarius*, a curious study on the possibility of expressing infinite sums by numerical denominations as in counting the sands of the universe, Archimedes writes:[13] "For you have known that the universe is called a sphere by several astrologers, its center the center of the earth, and its radius equal to a line drawn from the center of the sun to the center of the earth. This was written for the unlearned, as you have known from the astrologers.... [Aristarchus of Samos][14] concludes that the world is many times greater than the estimate we have just given. He supposes that the fixed stars and the sun remain motionless, but that the earth following a circular course, revolves around the sun as a center, and that the sphere of the fixed stars having the same sun as a center, is so vast that the circle which he supposes the earth to follow in revolving holds the same ratio to the distance of the fixed stars as the center of a sphere holds to its circumference."

These ancient philosophers realized in some degree the immensity of the universe in which the earth was but a point. They held that the earth was an unsupported sphere the size of which Eratosthenes (c. 276-194 B.C.) had calculated approximately. They knew the sun was far larger than the earth, and Cicero with other thinkers recognized the insignificance of earthly affairs in the face of such cosmic immensity. They knew too about the seven planets, had studied their orbits, and worked out astronomical ways of measuring the passage of time with a fair amount of accuracy. Hipparchus and other thinkers had discovered the fact of the precession of the equinoxes, though there was no adequate theory to account for it until Copernicus formulated his "motion of declination." The Pythagoreans accepted the idea of the earth's turning upon its axis, and some even held the idea of its revolution around the motionless sun. Others suggested that comets had orbits which they uniformly followed and therefore their reappearance could be anticipated. [15]

Why then was the heliocentric theory not definitely accepted?

In the first place, such a theory was contrary to the supposed facts of daily existence. A man did not have to be trained in the schools to observe that the earth seemed stable under his feet and that each morning the sun swept from the east to set at night in the west. Sometimes it rose more to the north or to the south than at other times. How could that be explained if the sun were stationary?

Study of the stars was valuable for navigators and for surveyors, perhaps, but such disturbing theories should not be propounded by philosophers. Cleanthes,[16] according to Plutarch,[17] "advised that the Greeks ought to have prosecuted Aristarchus the Samian for blasphemy against religion, as shaking the very foundations of the world, because this man endeavoring to save appearances, supposed that the heavens remained immovable and that the earth moved through an oblique circle, at the same time turning about its own axis." Few would care to face their fellows as blasphemers and impious thinkers on behalf of an unsupported theory. Eighteen hundred years later

Galileo would not do so, even though in his day the theory was by no means unsupported by observation.

Furthermore, one of the weaknesses of the Greek civilization militated strongly against the acceptance of this hypothesis so contrary to the evidence of the senses. Experimentation and the development of applied science was practically an impossibility where the existence of slaves made manual labor degrading and shameful. Men might reason indefinitely; but few, if any, were willing to try to improve the instruments of observation or to test their observations by experiments.

At the same time another astronomical theory was developing which was an adequate explanation for the phenomena observed up to that time. [18] This theory of epicycles and eccentrics worked out by Apollonius of Perga (c. 225 B.C.) and by Hipparchus (c. 160 B.C.) and crystallized for posterity in Ptolemy's great treatise on astronomy, the *Almagest*, (c. 140 A.D.) became the fundamental principle of the science until within the last three hundred years. The theory of the eccentric was based on the idea that heavenly bodies Following circular orbits revolved around a center that did not coincide with that of the observer on the earth. That would explain why the sun appeared sometimes nearer the earth and sometimes farther away. The epicycle represented the heavenly body as moving along the circumference of one circle (called the epicycle) the center of which moves on another circle (the deferent). With better observations additional epicycles and eccentric were used to represent the newly observed phenomena till in the later Middle Ages the universe became a

" − −Sphere
With Centric and Eccentric scribbled o'er,
Cycle and Epicycle, Orb in Orb" − [19]

Yet the heliocentric theory was not forgotten. Vitruvius, a famous Roman architect of the Augustan Age, discussing the system of the universe, declared that Mercury and Venus, the planets nearest the sun, moved around it as their center, though the earth was the center of the universe.[20] This same notion recurs in Martianus Capella's book[21] in the fifth century A.D. and again, somewhat modified, in the 16th century in Tycho Brahe's conception of the universe.

Ptolemy devotes a column or two of his *Almagest* [22] (to use the familiar Arabic name for his *Syntaxis Mathematica*) to the refutation of the heliocentric theory, thereby preserving it for later ages to ponder on and for a Copernicus to develop. He admits at the outset that such a theory is only tenable for the stars and their phenomena, and he gives at least three reasons why it is ridiculous. If the earth were not at the center, the observed facts of the seasons and of day and night would be disturbed and even upset. If the earth moves, its vastly greater mass would gain in speed upon other bodies, and soon animals and other lighter bodies would be left behind unsupported in the air—a notion "ridiculous to the last degree," as he comments, "even to imagine it." Lastly, if it moves, it would have such tremendous velocity that stones or arrows shot straight up in the air must fall to the ground east of their starting point,—a "laughable supposition" indeed to Ptolemy.

This book became the great text of the Middle Ages; its author's name was given to the geocentric theory it maintained. Astronomy for a thousand years was valuable only to determine the time of Easter and other festivals of the Church, and to serve as a basis for astrology for the mystery-loving people of Europe.

To the Arabians in Syria and in Spain belongs the credit of preserving for Europe during this long period the astronomical works of the Greeks, to which they added their own valuable observations of the heavens—valuable because made with greater skill and better instruments,[23] and because with these observations later scientists could illustrate the permanence or the variability of important elements. They also discovered the so-called "trepidation" or apparent shifting of the fixed stars to explain which they added another sphere to Ptolemy's eight. Early in the sixth century Uranus translated Aristotle's works into Syrian, and this later was translated into Arabic.[24] Albategnius[25] (c. 850-829 A.D.), the Arabian prince who was the greatest of all their astronomers, made his observations from Aracte and Damascus, checking up and in some cases amending Ptolemy's results.[26]

Then the center of astronomical development shifted from Syria to Spain and mainly through this channel passed on into Western Europe. The scientific fame of Alphonse X of Castile (1252-1284 A.D.) called the Wise, rests chiefly upon his encouragement of astronomy. With his support the Alfonsine Tables were calculated. He is said[27] to have summoned fifty learned men from Toledo, Cordova and Paris to translate into Spanish the works of Ptolemy and other philosophers. Under his patronage the University of Salamanca developed rapidly to become within two hundred years one of the four great universities of Europe[28]—a center for students from all over Europe and the headquarters for new thought, where Columbus was sheltered,[29] and later the Copernican system was accepted and publicly taught at a time when Galileo's views were suppressed.[30]

Popular interest in astronomy was evidently aroused, for Sacrobosco (to give John Holywood[31] his better known Latin name) a Scotch professor at the Sorbonne in Paris in the 13th century, published a small treatise *De Sphæri Mundo* that was immensely popular for centuries,[32] though it was practically only an abstract of the *Almagest*. Whewell[33] tells of a French poem of the time of Edward I entitled *Ymage du Monde*, which gave the Ptolemaic view and was illustrated in the manuscript in the University of Cambridge with a picture of the spherical earth with men upright on it at every point, dropping balls down perforations in the earth to illustrate the tendency of all things toward the center. Of the same period (13th century) is an Arabian compilation in which there is a reference to another work, the book of Hammarmunah the Old, stating that "the earth turns upon itself in the form of a circle, and that some are on top, the others below ... and there are countries in which it is constantly day or in which at least the night continues only some instants."[34] Apparently, however, such advanced views were of no influence, and the Ptolemaic theory remained unshaken down to the close of the 15th century.

Aside from the adequacy of this explanation of the universe for the times, the attitude of the Church Fathers on the matter was to a large degree responsible for this acquiescence. Early in the first century A.D., Philo Judæus[35] emphasized the minor importance of visible objects compared with intellectual matters, — a foundation stone in the Church's theory of an homocentric universe. Clement of Alexandria (c. 150 A.D.) calls the heavens solid since what is solid is capable of being perceived by the senses.[36] Origen (c. 185-c. 254.) has recourse to the Holy Scriptures to support his notion that the sun, moon, and stars are living beings obeying God's commands. [37] Then Lactantius thunders against those who discuss the universe as comparable to people discussing "the character of a city they have never seen, and whose name only they know." "Such matters cannot be found out by inquiry."[38] The existence of the antipodes and the rotundity of the earth are "marvelous fictions," and philosophers are "defending one absurd opinion by another"[39] when in explanation why bodies would not fall off a spherical earth, they claim these are borne to the center.

How clearly even this brief review illustrates what Henry Osborn Taylor calls[40] the fundamental principles of patristic faith: that the will of God is the one cause of all things (voluntate Dei immobilis manet et stat in sæculum terra.[41] Ambrose: *Hexæmeron.*) and that this will is unsearchable. He further points out that Augustine's and Ambrose's sole interest in natural fact is as "confirmatory evidence of Scriptural truth." The great Augustine therefore denies the existence of antipodes since they could not be peopled by Adam's children.[42] He indifferently remarks elsewhere:[43] "What concern is it to me whether the heavens as a sphere enclose the earth in the middle of the world or overhang it on either side?" Augustine does, however, dispute the claims of astrologers accurately to foretell the future by the stars, since the fates of twins or those born at the same moment are so diverse.[44]

Philastrius (d. before 397 A.D.) dealing with various heresies, denounces those who do not believe the stars are fixed in the heavens as "participants in the vanity of pagans and the foolish opinions of philosophers," and refers to the widespread idea of the part the angels play in guiding and impelling the heavenly bodies in their courses.[45]

It would take a brave man to face such attitudes of scornful indifference on the one hand and denunciation on the other, in support of a theory the Church considered heretical.

Meanwhile the Church was developing the homocentric notion which would, of course, presuppose the central position in the universe for man's abiding place. In the pseudo-Dionysius[46] is an elaborately worked out hierarchy of the beings in the universe that became the accepted plan of later centuries, best known to modern times through Dante's blending of it with the Ptolemaic theory in the *Divine Comedy*.[47] Isidore of Seville taught that the universe was created to serve man's purposes,[48] and Peter Lombard (12th cent.) sums up the situation in the definite statement that man was placed at the center of the universe to be served by that universe and in turn himself to serve God.[49] Supported by the mighty Thomas Aquinas[50] this became a fundamental Church doctrine.

An adequate explanation of the universe existed. Aristotle, Augustine, and the other great authorities of the Middle Ages, all upheld the conception of a central earth encircled by the seven planetary spheres and by the all embracing starry firmament. In view of the phrases used in the Bible about the heavens, and in view of the formation of fundamental theological doctrines based on this supposition by the Church Fathers, is it surprising that any other than a geocentric theory seemed untenable, to be dismissed with a smile when not denounced as heretical? Small wonder is it, in the absence of the present day mechanical devices for the exact measurement of time and space as aids to observation, that the Ptolemaic, or geocentric, theory of the universe endured through centuries as it did, upheld by the authority both of the Church and, in essence at least, by the great philosophers whose works constituted the teachings of the schools.

# CHAPTER II.
## COPERNICUS AND HIS TIMES.

DURING these centuries, one notable scholar at least stood forth in open hostility to the slavish devotion to Aristotle's writings and with hearty appreciation for the greater scientific accuracy of "infidel philosophers among the Arabians, Hebrews and Greeks."[51] In his *Opus Tertium* (1267), Roger Bacon also pointed out how inaccurate were the astronomical tables used by the Church, for in 1267, according to these tables "Christians will fast the whole week following the true Easter, and will eat flesh instead of fasting at Quadragesima for a week—which is absurd," and thus Christians are made foolish in the eyes of the heathen.[52] Even the rustic, he added, can observe the phases of the moon occurring a week ahead of the date set by the calendar.[53] Bacon's protests were unheeded, however, and the Church continued using the old tables which grew increasingly inaccurate with each year. Pope Sixtus IV sought to reform the calendar two centuries later with the aid of Regiomontanus, then the greatest astronomer in Europe (1475);[54] the Lateran Council appealed to Copernicus for help (1514), but little could be done, as Copernicus replied, till the sun's and the moon's positions had been observed far more precisely;[55] and the modern scientific calendar was not adopted until 1582 under Pope Gregory XIII.

-21

What was the state of astronomy in the century of Copernicus's birth? Regiomontanus—to use Johann Müller's Latin name—his teacher Pürbach, and the great cardinal Nicolas of Cues were the leading astronomers of this fifteenth century. Pürbach[56] (1432-1462) died before he had fulfilled the promise of his youth, leaving his *Epitome of Ptolemy's Almagest* to be completed by his greater pupil. In his *Theorica Planetarum* (1460) Pürbach sought to explain the motions of the planets by placing each planet between the walls of two curved surfaces with just sufficient space in which the planet could move. As M. Delambre remarked:[57] "These walls might aid the understanding, but one must suppose them transparent; and even if they guided the planet as was their purpose, they hindered the movement of the comets. Therefore they had to be abandoned, and in our own modern physics they are absolutely superfluous; they have even been rather harmful, since they interfered with the slight irregularities caused by the force of attraction in planetary movements which observations have disclosed." This scheme gives some indication of the elaborate devices scholars evolved in order to cope with the increasing number of seeming irregularities observed in "the heavens," and perhaps it makes clearer why Copernicus was so dissatisfied with the astronomical hypothesis of his day, and longed for some simpler, more harmonious explanation.

Regiomontanus[58] (1436-1476) after Pürbach's death, continued his work, and his astronomical tables (pub. 1475) were in general use throughout Europe till superseded by the vastly more accurate Copernican Tables a century later. It has been said[59] that his fame inspired Copernicus (born three years before the other's death in 1476) to become as great an astronomer. M. Delambre hails him as the wisest astronomer Europe had yet produced[60] and certainly his renown was approached only by that of the great Cardinal.

Both Janssen,[61] the Catholic historian, and Father Hagen[62] of the Vatican Observatory, together with many other Catholic writers, claim that a hundred years before Copernicus, Cardinal Nicolas Cusanus[63] (c. 1400-1464) had the courage and independence to uphold the theory of the earth's motion and its rotation on its axis. As Father Hagen remarked: "Had Copernicus been aware of these assertions he would probably have been encouraged by them to publish his own monumental work." But the Cardinal stated these views of the earth's motions in a mystical, hypothetical way which seems to justify the marginal heading "Paradox" (in the edition of 1565). [64] And unfortunately for these writers, the Jesuit father, Riccioli, the official spokesman of that order in the 17th century after Galileo's condemnation, speaking of this paradox, called attention, also, to a passage in one of the Cardinal's sermons as indicating that the latter had perhaps "forgotten himself" in the *De Docta Ignorantia*, or that this paradox "was repugnant to him, or that he had thought better of it."[65] The passage he referred to is as follows: "Prayer is more powerful than all created things. Although angels, or some kind of beings, move the spheres, the Sun and the stars; prayer is more powerful than they are, since it impedes motion, as when the prayer of Joshua made the Sun stand still."[66] This may explain why Copernicus apparently disregarded the Cardinal's paradox, for he made no reference to it in his book; and the statement itself, to judge by the absence of contemporary comment, aroused no interest at the time. But of late years, the Cardinal's position as stated in the *De Docta Ignorantia* has been repeatedly cited as an instance of the Church's friendly attitude toward scientific thought,[67] to show that Galileo's condemnation was due chiefly to his "contumacy and disobedience."

Copernicus[68] himself was born in Thorn on February 19, 1473,[69] seven years after that Hansa town founded by the Teutonic Order in 1231 had come under the sway of the king of Poland by the Second Peace of Thorn.[70] His father,[71] Niklas Koppernigk, was a wholesale merchant of Cracow who had removed to Thorn before 1458, married Barbara Watzelrode of an old patrician Thorn family, and there had served as town councillor for nineteen years until his death in 1483.[72] Thereupon his mother's brother, Lucas Watzelrode, later bishop of Ermeland, became his guardian, benefactor and close friend.[73]

After the elementary training in the Thorn school,[74] the lad entered the university at Cracow, his father's former home, where he studied under the faculty of arts from 1491-1494.[75] Nowhere else north of the Alps at this time were mathematics and astronomy in better standing than at this university.[76] Sixteen teachers taught these subjects there during the years of Copernicus's stay, but no record exists of his work under any of them.[77] That he must have studied these two sciences there, however, is proved by Rheticus's remark in the *Narratio Prima* [78] that Copernicus, after leaving Cracow, went to Bologna to work with Dominicus Maria di Novara "non tarn discipulus quam adjutor." He left Cracow without receiving a degree,[79] returned to Thorn in 1494 when he and his family decided he should enter the Church after first studying in Italy.[80] Consequently he crossed the Alps in 1496 and was that winter matriculated at Bologna in the "German nation."[81] The following summer he received word of his appointment to fill a vacancy among the canons of the cathedral chapter at Ermeland where his uncle had been bishop since 1489.[82] He remained in Italy, however, about ten years altogether, studying civil law at Bologna, and canon law and medicine at Padua,[83] yet receiving his degree as doctor of canon law from the university of Ferrara in 1503.[84] He was also in Rome for several months during the Jubilee year, 1500.

At this period the professor of astronomy at Bologna was the famous teacher Dominicus Maria di Novara (1454-1504), a man "ingenio et animo liber" who dared to attack the immutability of the Ptolemaic system, since his own observations, especially of the Pole Star, differed by a degree and more from the traditional ones.[85] He dared to criticise the long accepted system and to emphasize the Pythagorean notion of the underlying harmony and simplicity in nature[86]; and from him Copernicus may have acquired these ideas, for whether they lived together or not in Bologna, they were closely associated. It was here, too, that Copernicus began his study of Greek which later was to be the means[87] of encouraging him in his own theorizing by acquainting him with the ancients who had thought along similar lines.

In the spring of the year (1501) following his visit to Rome,[88] Copernicus returned to the Chapter at Frauenburg to get further leave of absence to study medicine at the University of Padua.[89] Whether he received a degree at Padua or not and how long he stayed there are uncertain points.[90] He was back in Ermeland early in 1506.

His student days were ended. And now for many years he led a very active life, first as companion and assistant to his uncle the Bishop, with whom he stayed at Schloss Heilsberg till after the Bishop's death in 1512; then as one of the leading canons of the chapter at Frauenburg, where he lived most of the rest of his life.[91] As the chapter representative for five years (at intervals) he had oversight of the spiritual and temporal affairs of two large districts in the care of the chapter.[92] He went on various diplomatic and other missions to the King of Poland,[93] to Duke Albrecht of the Teutonic Order,[94] and to the councils of the German states.[95] He wrote a paper of considerable weight upon the much needed reform of the Prussian currency.[96] His skill as a physician was in demand not only in his immediate circle[97] but in adjoining countries, Duke Albrecht once summoning him to Königsberg to attend one of his courtiers.[98] He was a humanist as well as a Catholic Churchman, and though he did not approve of the Protestant Revolt, he favored reform and toleration.[99] Gassendi claims that he was also a painter, at least in his student days, and that he painted portraits well received by his contemporaries.[100] But his interest and skill in astronomy must have been recognized early in his life for in 1514 the committee of the Lateran Council in charge of the reform of the calendar summoned him to their aid.[101]

He was no cloistered monk devoting all his time to the study of the heavens, but a cultivated man of affairs, of recognized ability in business and statesmanship, and a leader among his fellow canons. His mathematical and astronomical pursuits were the occupations of his somewhat rare leisure moments, except perhaps during the six years with his uncle in the comparative freedom of the bishop's castle, and during the last ten or twelve years of his life, after his request for a coadjutor had resulted in lightening his duties. In his masterwork *De Revolutionibus* [102] there are recorded only 27 of his own astronomical observations, and these extend over the years from 1497 to 1529. The first was made at Bologna, the second at Rome in 1500, and seven of the others at Frauenburg, where the rest were also probably made. It is believed the greater part of the *De Revolutionibus* was written at Heilsburg[103] where Copernicus was free from his chapter duties, for as he himself says[104] in the Dedication to the Pope (dated 1543) his work had been formulated not merely nine years but for "more than three nines of years." It had not been neglected all this time, however, as the original MS. (now in the Prague Library) with its innumerable changes and corrections shows how continually he worked over it, altering and correcting the tables and verifying his statements.[105]

Copernicus was a philosopher.[106] He thought out a new explanation of the world machine with relatively little practical work of his own,[107] though we know he controlled his results by the accumulated observations of the ages.[108] His instruments were inadequate, inaccurate and out of date even in his time, for much better ones were then being made at Nürnberg[109]; and the cloudy climate of Ermeland as well as his own active career prevented him from the long-continued, painstaking observing, which men like Tycho Brahe were to carry on later. Despite such handicaps, because of his dissatisfaction with the complexities and intricacies of the Ptolemaic system and because of his conviction that the laws of nature were simple and harmonious, Copernicus searched the writings of the classic philosophers, as he himself tells us,[110] to see what other explanation of the universe had been suggested. "And I found first in Cicero that a certain Nicetas had thought the earth moved. Later in Plutarch I found certain others had been of the same opinion." He quoted the Greek referring to Philolaus the Pythagorean, Heraclides of Pontus, and Ecphantes the Pythagorean.[111] As a result he began to consider the mobility of the earth and found that such an explanation seemingly solved many astronomical problems with a simplicity and a harmony utterly lacking in the old traditional scheme. Unaided by a telescope, he worked out in part the right theory of the universe and for the first time in history placed all the then known planets in their true positions with the sun at the center. He claimed that the earth turns on its axis as it travels around the sun, and careens slowly as it goes, thus by these three motions explaining many of the apparent movements of the sun and the planets. He retained,[112] however, the immobile heaven of the fixed stars (though vastly farther off in order to account for the non-observance of any stellar parallax[113]), the "perfect" and therefore circular orbits of the planets, certain of the old eccentrics, and 34 new epicycles in place of all the old ones which he had cast aside.[114] He accepted the false notion of trepidation enunciated by the Arabs in the 9th century and later overthrown by Tycho Brahe.[115] His calculations were weak.[116] But his great book is a sane and modern work in an age of astrology and superstition.[117] His theory is a triumph of reason and imagination and with its almost complete independence of authority is perhaps as original a work as an human being may be expected to produce.

Copernicus was extremely reluctant to publish his book because of the misunderstandings and malicious attacks it would unquestionably arouse.[118] Possibly, too, he was thinking of the hostility already existing between himself and his Bishop, Dantiscus,[119] whom he did not wish to antagonize further. But his devoted pupil and friend, Rheticus, aided by Tiedeman Giese, Bishop of Culm and a lifelong friend, at length (1542) persuaded him.[120] So he entrusted the matter to Giese who passed it on to Rheticus, then connected with the University at Wittenberg as professor of mathematics.[121] Rheticus, securing leave of absence from Melancthon his superior, went to Nürnberg to supervise the printing.[122] This was done by Petrejus. Upon his return to Wittenberg, Rheticus left in charge Johann Schöner, a famous mathematician and astronomer, and Andreas Osiander, a Lutheran preacher interested in astronomy. The printed book[123] was placed in Copernicus's hands at Frauenburg on May 24th, 1543, as he lay dying of paralysis.[124]

Copernicus passed away that day in ignorance that his life's work appeared before the world not as a truth but as an hypothesis; for there had been inserted an anonymous preface "ad lectorem de hypothesibus huius opera" stating this was but another hypothesis for the greater convenience of astronomers.[125] "Neque enim necesse est eas hypotheses esse veras, imo ne verisimiles quidem, sed sufficit hoc unum, si calculum observationibus congruentem exhibeant."[126] For years Copernicus was thought to have written this preface to disarm criticism. Kepler sixty years later (1601) called attention to this error,[127] and quoted Osiander's letters to Copernicus and to Rheticus of May, 1541, suggesting that the system be called an hypothesis to avert attacks by theologians and Aristotelians. He claimed that Osiander had written the preface; but Kepler's article never was finished and remained unpublished till 1858.[128] Giese and Rheticus of course knew that the preface falsified Copernicus's work, and Giese, highly indignant at the "impiety" of the printer (who he thought had written it to save himself from blame) wrote Rheticus urging him to write another "præfatiunculus" purging the book of this falsehood.[129] This letter is dated July 26, 1543, and the book had appeared in April. Apparently nothing was done and the preface was accepted without further challenge.

It remains to ask whether people other than Copernicus's intimates had known of his theory before 1543. Peucer, Melancthon's nephew, declared Copernicus was famous by 1525,[130] and the invitation from the Lateran Council committee indicates his renown as early as 1514. In Vienna in 1873[131] there was found a *Commentariolus*, or summary of his great work,[132] written by Copernicus for the scholars friendly to him. It was probably written soon after 1530, and gives a full statement of his views following a series of seven axioms or theses summing up the new theory. This little book probably occasioned the order from Pope Clement VII in 1533 to Widmanstadt to report to him on the new scheme.[133] This Widmanstadt did in the papal gardens before the Pope with several of the cardinals and bishops, and was presented with a book as his reward.

In 1536, the Cardinal Bishop of Capua, Nicolas von Schönberg, apparently with the intent to pave the way for the theory at Rome, wrote for a report of it.[134] It is not known whether the report was sent, and the cardinal died the following year. But that Copernicus was pleased by this recognition is evident from the prominence he gave to the cardinal's letter, as he printed it in his book at the beginning, even before the dedication to the Pope.

The most widely circulated account at this time, however, was the *Narratio Prima*, a letter from Georg Joachim of Rhaetia (better known as Rheticus), written in October, 1539, from Frauenburg to Johann Schöner at Nürnberg. [135] Rheticus,[136] at twenty-five years of age professor of mathematics at Wittenberg, had gone uninvited to Frauenburg early that summer to visit Copernicus and learn for himself more in detail about this new system. This was rather a daring undertaking, for not only were Luther and Melancthon outspoken in their condemnation of Copernicus, but Rheticus was going from Wittenberg, the headquarters of the Lutheran heresy, into the bishopric of Ermeland where to the Bishop and the King his overlord, the very name of Luther was anathema. Nothing daunted, Rheticus departed for Frauenberg and could not speak too highly of the cordial welcome he received from the old astronomer. He came for a few weeks, and remained two years to return to Wittenberg as an avowed believer in the system and its first teacher and promulgator. Not only did he write the *Narratio Prima* and an *Encomium Borussæ*, both extolling Copernicus, but what is more important, he succeeded in persuading him to allow the publication of the *De Revolutionibus*. Rheticus returned to his post in 1541, to resign it the next year and become Dean of the Faculty of Arts. In all probability the conflict was too intense between his new scientific beliefs and the statements required of him as professor of the old mathematics and astronomy.

His colleague, Erasmus Reinhold, continued to teach astronomy there, though he, too, accepted the Copernican system.[137] He published a series of tables (*Tabulæ Prutenicæ*, 1551) based on the Copernican calculations to supersede the inaccurate ones by Regiomontanus; and these were in general use throughout Europe for the next seventy-odd years. As he himself declared, the series was based in its principles and fundamentals upon the observations of the famous Nicolaus Copernicus. The almanacs deduced from these calculations probably did more to bring the new system into general recognition and gradual acceptance than did the theoretical works.[138]

Opposition to the theory had not yet gathered serious headway. There is record[139] of a play poking fun at the system and its originator, written by the Elbing schoolmaster (a Dutch refugee from the Inquisition) and given in 1531 by the villagers at Elbing (3 miles from Frauenburg). Elbing and Ermeland were hostile to each other, Copernicus was well known in Elbing though probably from afar, for there seems to have been almost no personal intercourse between canons and people, and the spread of Luther's teachings had intensified the hostility of the villagers towards the Church and its representatives. But not until Giordano Bruno made the Copernican system the starting-point of his philosophy was the Roman Catholic Church seriously aroused to combat it. Possibly Osiander's preface turned opposition aside, and certainly the non-acceptance of the system as a whole by Tycho Brahe, the leading astronomer of Europe at that time, made people slow to consider it.

# CHAPTER III.
# THE LATER DEVELOPMENT AND SCIENTIFIC DEFENSE OF THE COPERNICAN SYSTEM.

COPERNICUS accomplished much, but even his genius could not far outrun the times in which he lived. When one realizes that not only all the astronomers before him, but he and his immediate successor, Tycho Brahe, made all their observations and calculations unaided by even the simplest telescope, by logarithms or by pendulum clocks for accurate measurement of time,[140] one marvels not at their errors, but at the greatness of their genius in rising above such difficulties. This lack of material aids makes the work of Tycho Brahe,[141] accounted one of the greatest observers that has ever lived,[142] as notable in its way perhaps as that of Copernicus.

His life[143] was a somewhat romantic one. Born of noble family on December 14th, 1546, at Knudstrup in Denmark, Tyge Brahe, the second of ten children,[144] was early practically adopted by his father's brother. His family wished him to become a statesman and sent him in 1559 to the university at Copenhagen to prepare for that career. A partial eclipse of the sun on August 21st, 1560 as foretold by the astronomers thrilled the lad and determined him to study a science that could foretell the future and so affect men's lives.[145] When he was sent to Leipsic with a tutor in 1562 to study law, he devoted his time and money to the study of mathematics and astronomy. Two years later when eighteen years of age, he resolved to perform anew the task of Hipparchos and Ptolemy and make a catalogue of the stars more accurate than theirs. His family hotly opposed these plans; and for six years he wandered through the German states, now at Wittenberg, now at Rostock (where he fought the duel in which he lost part of his nose and had to have it replaced by one of gold and silver)[146] or at Augsburg—everywhere working on his chosen subjects. But upon his return to Denmark (1570) he spent two years on chemistry and medicine, till the startling appearance of the New Star in the constellation of Cassiopæa (November, 1572) recalled him to what became his life work.[147]

Through the interest and favor of King Frederick II, he was given the island of Hveen near Elsinore, with money to build an observatory and the pledge of an annual income from the state treasury for his support. [148] There at Uraniborg from 1576 to 1597 he and his pupils made the great catalogue of the stars, and studied comets and the moon. When he was forced to leave Hveen by the hostility and the economical tendencies of the young king,[149] after two years of wandering he accepted the invitation of the Emperor Rudolphus and established himself at Prague in Bohemia. Among his assistants at Prague was young Johann Kepler who till Tycho's death (on October 24, 1601) was his chief helper for twenty months, and who afterwards completed his observations, publishing the results in the Rudolphine Tables of 1627.

This "Phoenix among Astronomers" — as Kepler calls him,[150] — was the father of modern practical astronomy.[151] He also propounded a third system of the universe, a compromise between the Ptolemaic and the Copernican. In this the Tychonic system,[152] the earth is motionless and is the center of the orbits of the sun, the moon, and the sphere of the fixed stars, while the sun is the center of the orbits of the five planets.[153] Mercury and Venus move in orbits with radii shorter than the sun's radius, and the other three planets include the earth within their circuits. This system was in harmony with the Bible and accounted as satisfactorily by geometry as either of the other two systems for the observed phenomena.[154] To Tycho Brahe, the Ptolemaic system was too complex,[155] and the Copernican absurd, the latter because to account for the absence of stellar parallax it left vacant and purposeless a vast space between Saturn and the sphere of the fixed stars,[156] and because Tycho's observations did not show any trace of the stellar parallax that must exist if the earth moves.[157]

Though Tycho thus rejected the Copernican theory, his own proved to be the stepping stone toward the one he rejected,[158] for by it and by his study of comets he completely destroyed the ideas of solid crystalline spheres to the discredit of the scholastics; and his promulgation of a third theory of the universe helped to diminish men's confidence in authority and to stimulate independent thinking.

Copernicus worked out his system by mathematics with but slight aid from his own observations. It was a theory not yet proven true. Tycho Brahe, though denying its validity, contributed in his mass of painstaking, accurate observations the raw material of facts to be worked up by Kepler into the great laws of the planets attesting the fundamental truth of the Copernican hypothesis.

Johann Kepler[159] earned for himself the proud title of "lawmaker for the universe" in defiance of his handicaps of ill-health, family troubles, and straitened finances.[160] Born in Weil, Wurtemberg, (December 27, 1571) of noble but indigent parents, he was a sickly child unable for years to attend school regularly. He finally left the monastery school in Mulifontane in 1586 and entered the university at Tübingen to stay for four and a half years. There he studied philosophy, mathematics, and theology (he was a Lutheran) receiving the degree of Master of Arts in 1591. While at the university he studied under Mæstlin, professor of mathematics and astronomy, and a believer in the Copernican theory. Because of Mæstlin's teaching Kepler developed into a confirmed and enthusiastic adherent to the new doctrine.

In 1594 he reluctantly abandoned his favorite study, philosophy, and accepted a professorship in mathematics at Grætz in Styria. Two years later he published his first work: *Prodromus Dissertationum continens mysterium cosmographicum* etc. (1596) in which he sought to prove that the Creator in arranging the universe had thought of the five regular bodies which can be inscribed in a sphere according to which He had regulated the order, the number and the proportions of the heavens and their movements.[161] The book is important not only because of its novelty, but because it gave the Copernican doctrine public explanation and defense.[162] Kepler himself valued it enough to reprint it with his *Harmonia Mundi* twenty-five years later. And it won for him appreciative letters from various scientists, notably from Tycho Brahe and Galileo.[163]

As Kepler, a Lutheran, was having difficulties in Grætz, a Catholic city, he finally accepted Tycho's urgent invitation to come to Prague.[164] He came early in 1600, and after some adjustments had been made between the two,[165] he and his family settled with Tycho that autumn to remain till the latter's death the following November. Kepler himself then held the office of imperial mathematician by appointment for many years thereafter.[166]

With the researches of Tycho's lifetime placed at his disposal, Kepler worked out two of his three great planetary laws from Tycho's observations of the planet Mars. Yet, as M. Bertrand remarks,[167] it was well for Kepler that his material was not too accurate or its variations (due to the then unmeasured force of attraction) might have hindered him from proving his laws; and luckily for him the earth's orbit is so nearly circular that in calculating the orbit of Mars to prove its elliptical form, he could base his work on the earth's orbit as a circle without vitiating his results for Mars. [168] That a planet's orbit is an ellipse and not the perfect circle was of course a triumph for the new science over the scholastics and Aristotelians. But they had yet to learn what held the planets in their courses.

From Kepler's student days under Mæstlin when as the subject of his disputation he upheld the Copernican theory, to his death in 1630, he was a staunch supporter of the new teaching.[169] In his *Epitome Astronomiæ Copernicanæ* (1616) he answered objections to it at length.[170] He took infinite pains to convert his friends to the new system. It was in vain that Tycho on his deathbed had urged Kepler to carry on their work not on the Copernican but on the Tychonic scheme.[171]

Kepler had reasoned out according to physics the laws by which the planets moved.[172] In Italy at this same time Galileo with his optic tube (invented 1609) was demonstrating that Venus had phases even as Copernicus had declared, that Jupiter had satellites, and that the moon was scarred and roughened — ocular proof that the old system with its heavenly perfection in number (7 planets) and in appearance must be cast aside. Within a year after Galileo's death Newton was born[173] (January 4, 1643). His demonstration of the universal application of the law of gravitation (1687) was perhaps the climax in the development of the Copernican system. Complete and final proof was adding in the succeeding years by Roemer's (1644-1710) discovery of the velocity of light, by Bradley's (1693-1762) study of its aberration,[174] by Bessel's discovery of stellar parallax in 1838,[175] and by Foucault's experimental demonstration of the earth's axial motion with a pendulum in 1851.[176]

# PART TWO THE RECEPTION OF THE COPERNICAN THEORY.

## CHAPTER I.
## OPINIONS AND ARGUMENTS IN THE SIXTEENTH CENTURY.

DURING the lifetime of Copernicus, Roman Catholic churchmen had been interested in his work: Cardinal Schönberg wrote for full information, Widmanstadt reported on it to Pope Clement VII and Copernicus had dedicated his book to Pope Paul III.[177] But after his death, the Church authorities apparently paid little heed to his theory until some fifty years later when Giordano Bruno forced it upon their attention in his philosophical teachings. Osiander's preface had probably blinded their eyes to its implications.

The Protestant leaders were not quite so urbane in their attitude. While Copernicus was still alive, Luther is reported[178] to have referred to this "new astrologer" who sought to prove that the earth and not the firmament swung around, saying: "The fool will overturn the whole science of astronomy. But as the Holy Scriptures state, Joshua bade the sun stand still and not the earth." Melancthon was more interested in this new idea, perhaps because of the influence of Rheticus, his colleague in the University of Wittenberg and Copernicus's great friend and supporter; but he too preferred not to dissent from the accepted opinion of the ages.[179] Informally in a letter to a friend he implies the absurdity of the new teaching,[180] and in his *Initia Doctrinæ Physicæ* he goes to some pains to disprove the new assumption not merely by mathematics but by the Bible, though with a kind of apology to other physicists for quoting the Divine Witness.[181] He refers to the phrase in Psalm XIX likening the sun in its course "to a strong man about to run a race," proving that the sun moves. Another Psalm states that the earth was founded not to be moved for eternity, and a similar phrase occurs in the first chapter of Ecclesiastes. Then there was the miracle when Joshua bade the sun stand still. While this is a sufficient witness to the truths there are other proofs: First, in the turning of a circumference, the center remains motionless. Next, changes in the length of the day and of the seasons would ensue, were the position of the earth in the universe not central, and it would not be equidistant from the two poles. (He has previously disposed of infinity by stating that the heavens revolve around the pole, which could not happen if a line drawn from the center of the universe were infinitely projected).[182] Furthermore, the earth must be at the center for its shadow to fall upon the moon in an eclipse. He refers next to the Aristotelian statement that to a simple body belongs one motion: the earth is a simple body; therefore it can have but one motion. What is true of the parts applies to the whole; all the parts of the earth are borne toward the earth and there rest; therefore the whole earth is at rest. Quiet is essential to growth. Lastly, if the earth moved as fast as it must if it moves at all, everything would fly to pieces.[183]

Melancthon thus sums up the usual arguments from the Scriptures, from Aristotle, Ptolemy and the then current physics, in opposition to this theory. Not only did he publish his own textbook on physics, but he republished Sacrobosco's famous introduction to astronomy, writing for it a preface urging diligent study of this little text endorsed by so many generations of scholars.

Calvin, the great teacher of the Protestant Revolt, apparently was little touched by this new intellectual current.[184] He did write a semi-popular tract[185] against the so called "judicial" astrology, then widely accepted, which he, like Luther, condemns as a foolish superstition, though he values "la vraie science d'astrologie" from which men understand not merely the order and place of the stars and planets, but the causes of things. In his *Commentaries*, he accepts the miracle of the sun's standing still at Joshua's command as proof of the faith Christ commended, so strong that it will remove mountains; and he makes reference only to the time-honored Ptolemaic theory in his discussion of Psalm XIX.[186]

For the absolute authority of the Pope the Protestant leaders substituted the absolute authority of the Bible. It is not strange, then, that they ignored or derided a theory as yet unsupported by proof and so difficult to harmonize with a literally accepted Bible.

How widespread among the people generally did this theory become in the years immediately following the publication of the *De Revolutionibus*? M. Flammarion, in his *Vie de Copernic* (1872), refers[187] to the famous clock in the Strasburg Cathedral as having been constructed by the University of Strasburg in protest against the action taken by the Holy Office against Galileo, (though the clock was constructed in 1571 and Galileo was not condemned until 1633). This astronomical clock constructed only thirty years after the death of Copernicus, he claims represented the Copernican system of the universe with the planets revolving around the sun, and explained clearly in the sight of the people what was the thought of the makers. Lest no one should miscomprehend, he adds, the portrait of Copernicus was placed there with this inscription: Nicolai Copernici vera effigies, ex ipsius autographo depicta.

This would be important evidence of the spread of the theory were it true. But M. Flammarion must have failed to see a brief description of the Strasburg Clock written in 1856 by Charles Schwilgué, son of the man who renovated its mechanism in 1838-1842. He describes the clock as it was before his father made it over and as it is today. Originally constructed in 1352, it was replaced in 1571 by an astrolabe based on the Ptolemaic system; six hands with the zodiacal signs of the planets gave their daily movements and, together with a seventh representing the sun, revolved around a map of the world.[188] When M. Schwilgué repaired the clock in 1838, he changed it to harmonize with the Copernican system.[189]

But within eighteen years after the publication of the *De Revolutionibus*, proof of its influence is to be found in such widely separated places as London and the great Spanish University of Salamanca. In 1551, Robert Recorde, court physician to Edward and to Mary and teacher of mathematics, published in London his *Castle of Knowledge*, an introduction to astronomy and the first book printed in England describing the Copernican system.[190] He evidently did not consider the times quite ripe for a full avowal of his own allegiance to the new doctrine, but the remarks of the *Maister* and the *Scholler* are worth repeating:[191]

> "Maister: ... howbeit Copernicus a man of great learning, of much experience, and of wonderfull diligence in observation, hath renewed the opinion of Aristarchus Samius, affirming that the earth, not onely moveth circularly about his owne centre, but also may be, yea and is, continually out of the precise centre of the world eight and thirty hundred thousand miles: but because the understanding of that controversie depends of profounder knowledge than in this Introduction may be uttered conveniently, I wil let it passe til some other time.

> "Scholler: Nay sit, in good faith, I desire not to heare such vaine fantasies, so farre against the common reason, and repugnant to the content of all the learned multitude of Writers, and therefore let it passe for ever and a day longer.

> "Maister: You are too yong to be a good judge in so great a matter: it passeth farre your learning, and their's also, that are much better learned than you, to improuve his supposition by good arguments, and therefore you were best condemne nothing that you do not well understand: but an other time, as I saide, I will so declare his supposition, that you shall not onely wonder to heare it, but also peradventure be as earnest then to credite it, as you are

now to condemne it: in the meane season let us proceed forward in our former order...."

This little book, reprinted in 1556 and in 1596, and one of the most popular of the mathematical writings in England during that century, must have interested the English in the new doctrine even before Bruno's emphatic presentation of it to them in the eighties.

Yet the English did not welcome it cordially. One of the most popular books of this period was Sylvester's translation (1591) of DuBartas's *The Divine Weeks* which appeared in France in 1578, a book loved especially by Milton.[192] DuBartas writes:[193]

"Those clerks that think — think how absurd a jest!
That neither heavens nor stars do turn at all,
Nor dance around this great, round earthly ball,
But the earth itself, this massy globe of our's,
Turns round about once every twice twelve hours!
And we resemble land-bred novices
New brought aboard to venture on the seas;
Who at first launching from the shore suppose
The ship stands still and that the firm earth goes."

Quite otherwise was the situation in the sixteenth century at the University of Salamanca. A new set of regulations for the University, drawn up at the King's order by Bishop Covarrubias, was published in 1561. It contained the provision in the curriculum that "Mathematics and Astrology are to be given in three years, the first, Astrology, the second, Euclid, Ptolemy or Copernicus *ad vota audientium*," which also indicates, as Vicente de la Fuente points out, that at this University "the choice of the subject-matter to be taught lay not with the teachers but with the students, a rare situation."[194] One wonders what happened there when the professors and students received word[195] from the Cardinal Nuncio at Madrid in 1633 that the Congregations of the Index had decreed the Copernican doctrine was thereafter in no way to be held, taught or defended.

One of the graduates of this University, Father Zuñiga,[196] (better known as Didacus à Stunica), wrote a commentary on Job that was licensed to be printed in 1579, but was not published until 1584 at Toledo. Another edition appeared at Rome seven years later. It evidently was widely read for it was condemned *donec corrigatur* by the Index in 1616 and the mathematical literature of the next half century contains many allusions to his remarks on Job: IX: 6; "Who shaketh the earth out of her place, and the pillars thereof tremble." After commenting here upon the greater clarity and simplicity of the Copernican theory, Didacus à Stunica then states that the theory is not contradicted by Solomon in Ecclesiastes, as that "text signifieth no more but this, that although the succession of ages, and generations of men on earth be various, yet the earth itself is still one and the same, and continueth without any sensible variation" ... and "it hath no coherence with its context (as Philosophers show) if it be expounded to speak of the earth's immobility. The motion that belongs to the earth by way of speech is assigned to the sun even by Copernicus himself, and those who are his followers.... To conclude, no place can be produced out of Holy Scriptures which so clearly speaks the earth's immobility as this doth its mobility. Therefore this text of which we have spoken is easily reconciled to this opinion. And to set forth the wonderful power and wisdom of God who can indue the frame of the whole earth (it being of monstrous weight by nature) with motion, this our Divine pen-man added; 'And the pillars thereof tremble:' As if he would teach us, from the doctrine laid down, that it is moved from its foundations."[197]

French thinkers, like the English, did not encourage the new doctrine at this time. Montaigne[198] was characteristically indifferent: "What shall we reape by it, but only that we neede not care which of the two it be? And who knoweth whether a hundred yeares hence a third opinion will arise which happily shall overthrow these two præcedent?" The famous political theorist, Jean Bodin, (1530-1596), was as thoroughly opposed to it as DuBartas had been. In the last year of his life, Bodin wrote his *Universæ Naturæ Theatrum* [199] in which he discussed the origin and composition of the universe and of the animal, vegetable, mineral and spiritual kingdoms. These five books (or divisions) reveal his amazing ideas of geology, physics and astronomy while at the same time they show a mind thoroughly at home in Hebrew and Arabian literature as well as in the classics. His answer to the Copernican doctrine is worth quoting to illustrate the attitude of one of the keenest thinkers in a brilliant era:

"Theorist: Since the sun's heat is so intense that we read it has sometimes burned crops, houses and cities in Scythia,[200] would it not be more reasonable that the sun is still and the earth indeed revolves?

"Mystic: Such was the old idea of Philolaus, Timæus, Ecphantes, Seleucus, Aristarchus of Samos, Archimedes and Eudoxus, which Copernicus has renewed in our time. But it can easily be refuted by its shallowness although no one has done it thoroughly.

"The.: What arguments do they rely on who hold that the earth is revolved and that the sun forsooth is still?

"Mys.: Because the comprehension of the human mind cannot grasp the incredible speed of the heavenly spheres and especially of the tenth sphere which must be ten times greater than that of the eighth, for in twenty-four hours it must traverse 469,562,845 miles, so that the earth seems like a dot in the universe. This is the chief argument. Besides this, we get rid entirely of epicycles in representing the motions of the planets and what is taught concerning the motion of trepidation in the eighth sphere vanishes. Also, there is no need for the ninth and tenth spheres. There is one argument which they have omitted but which seems to me more efficacious than any, viz.: rest is nobler than movement, and that celestial and divine things have a stable nature while elemental things have motion, disturbance and unrest; therefore it seems more probable that the latter move rather than the former. But while serious absurdities result from the idea of Eudoxus, far more serious ones result from that of Copernicus.

"The.: What are these absurdities?

"Mys.: Eudoxus knew nothing of trepidation, so his idea seems to be less in error. But Copernicus, in order to uphold his own hypothesis, claims the earth has three motions, its diurnal and annual ones, and trepidation; if we add to these the pull of weight towards the center, we are attributing four natural motions to one and the same body. If this is granted, then the very foundations of physics must fall into ruins; for all are agreed upon this that each natural body has but one motion of its own, and that all others are said to be either violent or voluntary. Therefore, since he claims the earth is agitated by four motions, one only can be its own, the others must be confessedly violent; yet nothing violent in nature can endure continuously. Furthermore the earth is not moved by water, much less by the motion of air or fire in the way we have stated the heavens are moved by the revolutions of the enveloping heavens. Copernicus further does not claim that all the heavens are immobile but that some are moved, that is, the moon, Mercury, Venus, Mars, Jupiter and Saturn. But why such diversity? No one in his senses, or imbued with the slightest knowledge of physics, will ever think that the earth, heavy and unwieldy from its own weight and mass, staggers up and down around its own center and that of the sun; for at the slightest jar of the earth, we would see cities and fortresses, towns and mountains thrown down. A certain courtier Aulicus, when some astrologer in court was upholding Copernicus's idea before Duke Albert of Prussia, turning to the servant who was pouring the Falernian, said: "Take care that the flagon is not spilled."[201] For if the earth were to be moved, neither an arrow shot straight up, nor a stone dropped from the top of a tower would fall perpendicularly, but either ahead or behind. With this argument Ptolemy refuted Eudoxus. But if we search into the secrets of the Hebrews and penetrate their sacred sanctuaries, all these arguments can easily be confirmed; for when the Lord of Wisdom said the sun swept in its swift course from the eastern shore to the west, he added this: Terra vero stat æternam. Lastly, all things on finding places suitable to their natures, remain there, as Aristotle writes. Since therefore the earth has been alloted a place fitting its nature, it cannot be whirled around by other motion than its own.

"The.: I certainly agree to all the rest with you, but Aristotle's law I think involves a paralogism, for by this argument the heavens should be immobile since they are in a place fitting their nature.

"Mys.: You argue subtly indeed, but in truth this argument does not seem necessary to me; for what Aristotle admitted, that, while forsooth all the parts of the firmament changed their places, the firmament as a whole did not, is exceedingly absurd. For either the whole heaven is at rest or the whole heaven is moved. The senses themselves disprove that it is at rest; therefore it is moved. For it does not follow that if a body is not moved away from its place, it is not moved in that place. Furthermore, since we have the most certain proof of the movement of trepidation, not only all the parts of the firmament, but also the eight spheres, must necessarily leave their places and move up and down, forward and back."[202]

This was the opinion of a profound thinker and experienced man of affairs living when Tycho Brahe and Bruno were still alive and Kepler and Galileo were beginning their astronomical investigations. But he was not alone in his views, as we shall see; for at the close of the sixteenth century, the Copernican doctrine had few avowed supporters. The Roman Church was still indifferent; the Protestants clinging to the literal interpretation of the Bible were openly antagonistic; the professors as a whole were too Aristotelian to accept or pay much attention to this novelty, except Kepler and his teacher Mæstlin (though the latter refused to uphold it in his textbook);[203] while astronomers and mathematicians who realized the insuperable objections to the Ptolemaic conception, welcomed the Tychonic system as a *via media*; and the common folk, if they heard of it at all, must have ridiculed it because it was so plainly opposed to what they saw in the heavens every day. In the same way their intellectual superiors exclaimed at the "delirium" of those supporting such a notion.[204] One thinker, however was to see far more in the doctrine than Copernicus himself had conceived, and by Giordano Bruno the Roman Church was to be aroused.

# CHAPTER II.
## BRUNO AND GALILEO.

WHEN the Roman Catholic authorities awoke to the dangers of the new teaching, they struck with force. The first to suffer was the famous monk-philosopher, Giordano Bruno, whose trial by the Holy Office was premonitory of trouble to come for Galileo.[205]

After an elementary education at Naples near his birth-place, Nola,[206] Filippo Bruno[207] entered the Dominican monastery in 1562 or 1563 when about fourteen years old, assuming the name Giordano at that time. Before 1572, when he entered the priesthood, he had fully accepted the Copernican theory which later became the basis of all his philosophical thought. Bruno soon showed he was not made for the monastic life. Various processes were started against him, and fleeing to Rome he abandoned his monk's garments and entered upon the sixteen years of wandering over Europe, a peripatetic teacher of the philosophy of an infinite universe as deduced from the Copernican doctrine and thus in a way its herald.[208] He reached Geneva in 1579 (where he did not accept Calvinism as was formerly thought),[209] but decided before many months had passed that it was wise to depart elsewhere because of the unpleasant position in which he found himself there. He had been brought before the Council for printing invectives against one of the professors, pointing out some twenty of his errors. The Council sent him to the Consistory, the governing body of the church, where a formal sentence of excommunication was passed against him. When he apologized it was withdrawn. Probably a certain stigma remained, and he left Geneva soon thereafter with a warm dislike for Calvinism. After lecturing at the University of Toulouse he appeared in Paris in 1581, where he held an extraordinary readership. Two years later he was in England, for he lectured at Oxford during the spring months and defended the Copernican theory before the Polish prince Alasco during the latter's visit there in June.[210]

To Bruno belongs the glory of the first public proclamation in England of the new doctrine,[211] though only Gilbert[212] and possibly Wright seem to have accepted it at the time. Upon Bruno's return to London, he entered the home of the French ambassador as a kind of secretary, and there spent the happiest years of his life till the ambassador's recall in October, 1585. It was during this period that he wrote some of his most famous books. In *La Cena de la Ceneri* he defended the Copernican theory, incidentally criticising the Oxford dons most severely,[213] for which he apologized in *De la Causa, Principio et Uno*. He developed his philosophy of an infinite universe in *De l'Infinito e Mondi*, and in the *Spaccio de la Bestia Trionphante* "attacked all religions of mere credulity as opposed to religions of truth and deeds."[214] This last book was at once thought to be a biting attack upon the Roman Church and later became one of the grounds of the Inquisition's charges against him. During this time in London also, he came to know Sir Philip Sydney intimately, and Fulk Greville as well as others of that brilliant period. He may have known Bacon;[215] but it is highly improbable that he and Shakespeare met,[216] or that Shakespeare ever was influenced by the other's philosophy.[217]

Leaving Paris soon after his return thither, Bruno wandered into southern Germany. At Marburg he was not permitted to teach, but at Wittenberg the Lutherans cordially welcomed him into the university. After a stay of a year and a half, he moved on to Prague for a few months, then to Helmstadt, Frankfort and Zurich, and back to Frankfort again where, in 1591, he received an invitation from a young Venetian patrician, Mœcenigo, to come to Venice as his tutor. He re-entered Italy, therefore, in August, much to the amazement of his contemporaries. It is probable that Mœcenigo was acting for the Inquisition.[218] At any rate, he soon denounced Bruno to that body and in May, 1592, surrendered him to it.[219]

In his trial before the Venetian Inquisition,[220] Bruno told the story of his life and stated his beliefs in answer to the charges against him, based mainly on travesties of his opinions. In this statement as well as in *La Cena de le Ceneri*, and in *De Immenso et Innumerabilis*,[221] Bruno shows how completely he had not merely accepted the Copernican doctrine, but had expanded it far beyond its author's conception. The universe according to Copernicus, though vastly greater than that conceived by Aristotle and Ptolemy, was still finite because enclosed within the sphere of the fixed stars. Bruno declared that not only was the earth only a lesser planet, but "this world itself was merely one of an infinite number of particular worlds similar to this, and that all the planets and other stars are infinite worlds without number composing an infinite universe, so that there is a double infinitude, that of the greatness of the universe, and that of the multitude of worlds."[222] How important this would be to the Church authorities may be realized by recalling the patristic doctrine that the universe was created for man and that his home is its center. Of course their cherished belief must be defended from such an attack, and naturally enough, the Copernican doctrine as the starting point of Bruno's theory of an infinite universe was thus brought into question;[223] for, as

M. Berti has said,[224] Bruno's doctrine was equally an astro-theology or a theological astronomy.

The Roman Inquisition was not content to let the Venetian court deal with this arch heretic, but wrote in September, 1592, demanding his extradition. The Venetian body referred its consent to the state for ratification which the Doge and Council refused to grant. Finally, when the Papal Nuncio had represented that Bruno was not a Venetian but a Neapolitan, and that cases against him were still outstanding both in Naples and in Rome, the state consented, and in February of the next year, Bruno entered Rome, a prisoner of the Inquisition. Nothing further is known about him until the Congregations took up his case on February 4th, 1599. Perhaps Pope Clement had hoped to win back to the true faith this prince of heretics.[225] However Bruno stood firm, and early in the following year he was degraded, sentenced and handed over to the secular authorities, who burned him at the stake in the Campo di Fiori, February 17, 1600.[226] All his books were put on the Index by decree of February 8, 1600, (where they remain to this day), and as a consequence they became extremely rare. It is well to remember Bruno's fate, when considering Galileo's case, for Galileo[227] was at that time professor of mathematics in the university of Padua and fully cognizant of the event.

Galileo's father, though himself a skilled mathematician, had intended that his son (born at Pisa, February 15, 1564), should be a cloth-dealer, but at length permitted him to study medicine instead at the university of Pisa, after an elementary education at the monastery of Vallombrosa near Florence. At the Tuscan Court in Pisa, Galileo received his first lesson in mathematics, which thereupon became his absorbing interest. After nearly four years he withdrew from the university to Florence and devoted himself to that science and to physics. His services as a professor at this time were refused by five of the Italian universities; finally, in 1589, he obtained the appointment to the chair of physics at Pisa. He became so unpopular there, however, through his attacks on the Aristotelian physics of the day, that after three years he resigned and accepted a similar position at Padua.[228] He remained here nearly eighteen years till his longing for leisure in which to pursue his researches, and the patronage of his good friend, the Grand Duke of Tuscany, brought him a professorship at the university of Pisa again, this time without obligation of residence nor of lecturing. He took up his residence in Florence in 1610; and later (1626), purchased a villa at Arcetri outside the city, in order to be near the convent where his favorite daughter "Suor Maria Celeste" was a religious.[229]

During the greater part of his lectureship at Padua, Galileo taught according to the Ptolemaic cosmogony out of compliance with popular feeling, though himself a Copernican. In a letter to Kepler (August 4, 1597)

[230] he speaks of his entire acceptance of the new system for some years; but not until after the appearance of the New Star in the heavens in 1604 and 1605, and the controversy that its appearance aroused over the Aristotelian notion of the perfect and unchangeable heavens, did he publicly repudiate the old scheme and teach the new. The only information we have as to how he came to adopt the Copernican scheme for himself is the account given by "*Sagredo*," Galileo's spokesman in the famous *Dialogue on the Two Principal Systems* (1632):

"Being very young and having scarcely finished my course of Philosophy which I left off, as being set upon other employments, there chanced to come into these parts a certain foreigner of Rostock, whose name as I remember, was Christianus Vurstitius, a follower of Copernicus, who in an Academy made two or three lectures upon this point, to whom many flock't as auditors; but I thinking they went more for the novelty of the subject than otherwise, did not go to hear him; for I had concluded with myself that that opinion could be no other than a solemn madnesse. And questioning some of those who had been there, I perceived they all made a jest thereof, except one, who told me that the business was not altogether to be laugh't at, and because this man was reputed by me to be very intelligent and wary, I repented that I was not there, and began from that time forward as oft as I met with anyone of the Copernican persuasion, to demand of them, if they had always been of the same judgment; and of as many as I examined, I found not so much as one, who told me not that he had been a long time of the contrary opinion, but to have changed it for this, as convinced by the reasons proving the same: and afterwards questioning them, one by one, to see whether they were well possest of the reasons of the other side, I found them all to be very ready and perfect in them; so that I could not truly say that they had took up this opinion out of ignorance, vanity, or to show the acuteness of their wits. On the contrary, of as many of the Peripateticks and Ptolemeans as I have asked (and out of curiosity I have talked with many) what pains they had taken in the Book of Copernicus, I found very few that had so much as superficially perused it: but of those whom, I thought, had understood the same, not one; and moreover, I have enquired amongst the followers of the Peripatetick Doctrine, if ever any of them had held the contrary opinion, and likewise found that none had. Whereupon considering that there was no man who followed the opinion of Copernicus that had not been first on the contrary side, and that was not very well acquainted with the reasons of Aristotle and Ptolemy; and on the contrary, that there is not one of the followers of Ptolemy that had ever been of the judgment of Copernicus, and that had left that to embrace this of Aristotle, considering, I say, these things, I began to think that one, who leaveth an opinion imbued with his milk, and followed by very many, to take up another owned by very few, and denied by all the Schools, and that really seems a very great Parodox, must needs have been moved, not to say forced, by more powerful reasons. For this cause I am become very curious to dive, as they say, into the bottom of this business ... and bring myself to a certainty in this subject."[231]

Galileo's brilliant work in mechanics and his great popularity — for his lectures were thronged — combined with his skilled and witty attacks upon the accepted scientific ideas of the age, embittered and antagonized many who were both conservative and jealous.[232] The Jesuits particularly resented his influence and power, for they claimed the leadership in the educational world and were jealous of intruders. Furthermore, they were bound by the decree of the fiftieth General Congregation of their society in 1593 to defend Aristotle, a decree strictly enforced.[233] While a few of the Jesuits were friendly disposed to Galileo at first, the controversies in which he and they became involved and their bitter attacks upon him made him feel by 1633 that they were among his chief enemies.[234]

Early in 1609, Galileo heard a rumor of a spy-glass having been made in Flanders, and proceeded to work one out for himself according to the laws of perspective. The fifth telescope that he made magnified thirty diameters, and it was with such instruments of his own manufacture that he made in the next three years his famous discoveries: Jupiter's four satellites (which he named the Medicean Planets), Saturn's "tripartite" character (the rings were not recognized as such for several decades thereafter), the stars of the Milky Way, the crescent form of Venus, the mountains of the moon, many more fixed stars, and the spots on the sun. Popular interest waxed with each new discovery and from all sides came requests for telescopes; yet there were those who absolutely refused even to look through a telescope lest they be compelled to admit Aristotle was mistaken, and others claimed that Jupiter's moons were merely defects in the instrument. The formal announcement of the first of these discoveries was made in the *Sidereus Nuncius* (1610), a book that aroused no little opposition. Kepler, however, had it reprinted at once in Prague with a long appreciative preface of his own.[235]

The following March Galileo went to Rome to show his discoveries and was received with the utmost distinction by princes and church dignitaries alike. A commission of four scientific members of the Roman College had previously examined his claims at Cardinal Bellarmin's suggestion, and had admitted their truth. Now Pope Paul V gave him long audiences; the

Academia dei Lincei elected him a member, and everywhere he was acclaimed. Nevertheless his name appears on the secret books of the Holy Office as early as May of that year (1611).[236] Already he was a suspect.

His *Delle Macchie Solari* (1611) brought on a sharp contest over the question of priority of discovery between him and the Jesuit father, Christopher Scheiner of Ingolstadt, from which Galileo emerged victorious and more disliked than before by that order. Opposition was becoming active; Father Castelli, for instance, the professor of mathematics at Pisa and Galileo's intimate friend, was forbidden to discuss in his lectures the double motion of the earth or even to hint at its probability. This same father wrote to his friend early in December, 1613, to tell him of a dinner-table conversation on this matter at the Tuscan Court, then wintering at Pisa. Castelli told how the Dowager Grand Duchess Cristina had had her religious scruples aroused by a remark that the earth's motion must be wrong because it contradicted the Scriptures, a statement that he had tried to refute.[237] Galileo wrote in reply (December 21, 1613), the letter[238] that was to cause him endless trouble, in which he marked out the boundaries between science and religion and declared it a mistake to take the literal interpretation of passages in Scripture that were obviously written according to the understanding of the common people. He pointed out in addition how futile the miracle of the sun's standing still was as an argument against the Copernican doctrine for, even according to the Ptolemaic system, not the sun but the *primum mobile* must be stayed for the day to be lengthened.

Father Castelli allowed others to read and to copy this supposedly private letter; copies went from hand to hand in Florence and discussion ran high. On the fourth Sunday in December, 1614, Father Caccini of the Dominicans preached a sermon in the church of S.M. Novella on Joshua's miracle, in which he sharply denounced the Copernican doctrine taught by Galileo as heretical, so he believed.[239] The Copernicans found a Neapolitan Jesuit who replied to Caccini the following Sunday from the pulpit of the Duomo.[240]

In February (1615), came the formal denunciation of Galileo to the Holy Office at Rome by Father Lorini, a Dominican associate of Caccini's at the Convent San Marco. The father sent with his "friendly warning," a copy of the letter to Castelli charging that it contained "many propositions which were either suspect or temerarious," and, he added, "though the *Galileisti* were good Christians they were rather stubborn and obstinate in their opinions."[241] The machinery of the Inquisition began secretly to turn. The authorities failed to get the original of the letter, for Castelli had returned that to Galileo at the latter's request.[242] Pope Paul sent word to Father Caccini to appear before the Holy Office in Rome to depose on this matter of Galileo's errors "pro exoneratione suæ conscientiæ."[243] This he did "freely" in March and was of course sworn to secrecy. He named a certain nobleman, a Copernican, as the source of his information about Galileo, for he did not know the latter even by sight. This nobleman was by order of the Pope examined in November after some delay by the Inquisitor at Florence. His testimony was to the effect that he considered Galileo the best of Catholics.[244]

Meanwhile the Consultors of the Holy Office had examined Lorini's copy of the letter and reported the finding of only three objectionable places all of which, they stated, could be amended by changing certain doubtful phrases; otherwise it did not deviate from the true faith. It is interesting to note that the copy they had differed in many minor respects from the original letter, and in one place heightened a passage with which the Examiners found fault as imputing falsehood to the Scriptures although they are infallible.[245] Galileo's own statement ran that there were many passages in the Scriptures which according to the literal meaning of the words, "hanno aspetto diverso dal vero...." The copy read, "molte propositioni falso quanto al nudo senso delle parole."

Rumors of trouble reached Galileo and, urged on by his friends, in 1615 he wrote a long formal elaboration of the earlier letter, addressing this one to the Dowager Grand Duchess, but he had only added fuel to the fire. At the end of the year he voluntarily went to Rome, regardless of any possible danger to himself, to see if he could not prevent a condemnation of the doctrine. [246] It came as a decided surprise to him to receive an order to appear before Cardinal Bellarmin on February 26, 1616,[2] and there to learn that the Holy Office had already condemned it two days before. He was told that the Holy Office had declared: first, "that the proposition that the sun is the center of the universe and is immobile is foolish and absurd in philosophy and formally heretical since it contradicts the express words of the Scriptures in many places, according to the meaning of the words and the common interpretation and sense of the Fathers and the doctors of theology; and, secondly, that the proposition that the earth is not the center of the universe nor immobile receives the same censure in philosophy and in regard to its theological truth, it at least is erroneous in Faith."[247]

Exactly what was said at that meeting between the two men became the crucial point in Galileo's trial sixteen years later, hence a somewhat detailed study is important. At the meeting of the Congregation on February 25th, the Pope ordered Cardinal Bellarmin to summon Galileo and, in the presence of a notary and witnesses lest he should prove recusant, warn him to abandon the condemned opinion and in every way to abstain from teaching, defending or discussing it; if he did not acquiesce, he was to be imprisoned.[248] The Secret Archives of the Vatican contain a minute reporting this interview (dated February 26, 1616), in which the Cardinal is said to have ordered Galileo to relinquish this condemned proposition, "nec eam de cætero, quovis modo, teneat, doceat aut defendat, verbo aut scriptis," and that Galileo promised to obey.[249] Rumors evidently were rife in Rome at the time as to what had happened at this secret interview, for Galileo wrote to the Cardinal in May asking for a statement of what actually had occurred so that he might silence his enemies. The Cardinal replied:

"We, Robert Cardinal Bellarmin, having heard that Signor Galileo was calumniated and charged with having abjured in our hand, and also of being punished by salutary penance, and being requested to give the truth, state that the aforesaid Signor Galileo has not abjured in our hand nor in the hand of any other person in Rome, still less in any other place, so far as we know, any of his opinions and teachings, nor has he received salutary penance nor any other kind; but only was he informed of the declaration made by his Holiness and published by the Sacred Congregation of the Index, in which it is stated that the doctrine attributed to Copernicus, — that the earth moves around the sun and that the sun stands in the center of the world without moving from the east to the west, is contrary to the Holy Scriptures and therefore cannot be defended nor held (non si possa difendere né tenere). And in witness of this we have written and signed these presents with our own hand, this 26th day of May, 1616.

Robert Cardinal Bellarmin."[250]

Galileo's defense sixteen years later[251] was that he had obeyed the order as given him by the Cardinal and that he had not "defended nor held" the doctrine in his *Dialoghi* but had refuted it. The Congregation answered that he had been ordered not only not to hold nor defend, but also not to treat in any way (quovis modo) this condemned subject. When Galileo disclaimed all recollection of that phrase and produced the Cardinal's statement in support of his position, he was told that this document, far from lightening his guilt, greatly aggravated it since he had dared to deal with a subject that he had been informed was contrary to the Holy Scriptures.[252]

To return to 1616. On the third of March the Cardinal reported to the Congregation in the presence of the Pope that he had warned Galileo and that Galileo had acquiesced.[253] The Congregation then reported its decree suspending "until corrected" "Nicolai Copernici De Revolutionibus Orbium Cœlestium, et Didaci Astunica in Job," and prohibiting "Epistola Fratris Pauli Antonii Foscarini Carmelitæ," together with all other books dealing with this condemned and prohibited doctrine. The Pope ordered this decree to be published by the Master of the Sacred Palace, which was done two days later. [254] But this prohibition could not have been widely known for two or three years; the next year Mulier published his edition of the *De Revolutionibus* at Amsterdam without a word of reference to it; in 1618 Thomas Feyens, professor at Louvain, heard vague rumors of the condemnation and wondered if it could be true;[255] and the following spring Fromundus, also at Louvain and later a noted antagonist of the new doctrine, wrote to Feyens asking:

> "What did I hear lately from you about the Copernicans? That they have been condemned a year or two ago by our Holy Father, Pope Paul V? Until now I have known nothing about it; no more have this crowd of German and Italian scholars, very learned and, as I think, very Catholic, who admit with Copernicus that the earth is turned. Is it possible that after a lapse of time as considerable as this, we have nothing more than a rumor of such an event? I find it hard to believe, since nothing more definite has come from Italy. Definitions of this sort ought above all to be published in the universities where the learned men are to whom the danger of such an opinion is very great."[256]

Galileo meanwhile had retired to Florence and devoted himself to mechanical science, (of which his work is the foundation) though constantly harassed by much ill health and many family perplexities. At the advice of his friends, he allowed the attacks on the Copernican doctrine to go unanswered,[257] till with the accession to the papacy in 1623 of Cardinal Barberini, as Urban VIII, a warm admirer and supporter of his, he thought relief was in sight. He was further cheered by a conversation Cardinal di Zollern reported having had with Pope Urban, in which his Holiness had reminded the Cardinal how he (the Pope) had defended Copernicus in the time of Paul V, and asserted that out of just respect owed to the memory of Copernicus, if he had been pope then, he would not have permitted his opinion to be declared heretical.[258] Feeling that he now had friends in power, Galileo began his great work, *Dialogo sopra i Due Sistemi Massimi del Mondo*, a dialogue in four "days" in which three interlocutors discuss the arguments for and against the Copernican theory, though coming to no definite conclusion. Sagredo was an avowed Copernican and Galileo's spokesman, Salviati was openminded, and the peripatetic was Simplicio, appropriately named for the famous Sicilian sixth century commentator on Aristotle.[259]

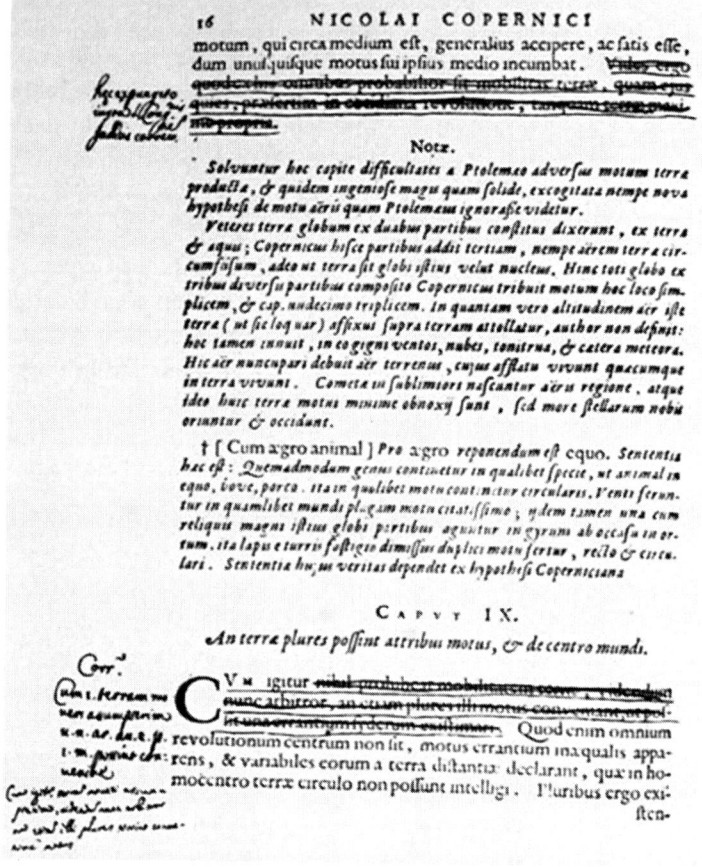

**A "Corrected" Page from the *De Revolutionibus*.**

A photographic facsimile (reduced) of a page from Mulier's edition (1617) of the *De Revolutionibus* as "corrected" according to the *Monitum* of the Congregations in 1620. The first writer underlined the passages to be deleted or altered with marginal notes indicating the changes ordered; the second writer scratched out these passages, and wrote out in full the changes the other had given in abbreviated form. The *Notæ* are Mulier's own, and so were not affected by the order. The effect of the page is therefore somewhat contradictory!

In 1630 he brought the completed manuscript to Riccardi, Master of the Sacred Palace, for permission to print it in Rome. After much reading and re-reading of it both by Riccardi and his associate, Father Visconti, permission was at length granted on condition that he insert a preface and a conclusion practically dictated by Riccardi, emphasizing its hypothetical character. [260] The Pope's own argument was to be used: "God is all-powerful; all things are therefore possible to Him; ergo, the tides cannot be adduced as a necessary proof of the double motion of the earth without limiting God's omnipotence—which is absurd."[261] Galileo returned to Florence in June with the permission to print his book in Rome. Meanwhile the plague broke out. He decided to print it in Florence instead, and on writing to Riccardi for that permission, the latter asked for the book to review it again. The times were too troublesome to risk sending it, so a compromise was finally effected: Galileo was to send the preface and conclusion to Rome and Riccardi agreed to instruct the Inquisitor at Florence as to his requirements and to authorize him to license the book.[262] The parts were not returned from Rome till July, 1631, and the book did not appear till February of the following year, when it was published at Florence with all these licenses, both the Roman and the Florentine ones.

The *Dialogo* was in Italian so that all could read it. It begins with an outline of the Aristotelian system, then points out the resemblances between the earth and the planets. The second "day" demonstrates the daily rotation of the earth on its axis. The next claims that the necessary stellar parallax is too minute to be observed and discusses the earth's annual rotation. The last seeks to prove this rotation by the ebb and flow of the tides. It is a brilliant book and received a great reception.

The authorities of the Inquisition at once examined it and denounced Galileo (April 17, 1633) because in it he not merely taught and defended the "condemned doctrine but was gravely suspected of firm adherence to this opinion."[263] Other charges made against him were that he had printed the Roman licenses without the permission of the Congregation, that he had printed the preface in different type so alienating it from the body of the book, and had put the required conclusion into the mouth of a fool (Simplicio), that in many places he had abandoned the hypothetical treatment and asserted the forbidden doctrine, and that he had dealt indecisively with the matter though the Congregation had specifically condemned the Copernican doctrine as contrary to the express words of the Scripture.[264]

The Pope became convinced that Galileo had ridiculed him in the character of Simplicio to whom Galileo had naturally enough assigned the Pope's syllogistic argument. On the 23rd of September, he ordered the

Inquisitor of Florence to notify Galileo (in the presence of concealed notary and witnesses in case he were "recusant") to come to Rome and appear before the Sacred Congregation before the end of the next month;[265] the publication and sale of the *Dialogo* meanwhile being stopped at great financial loss to the printer.[266] Galileo promised to obey; but he was nearly seventy years old and so much broken in health that a long difficult journey in the approaching winter seemed a great and unnecessary hardship, especially as he was loath to believe that the Church authorities were really hostile to him. Delays were granted him till the Pope in December finally ordered him to be in Rome within a month.[267] The Florentine Inquisitor replied that Galileo was in bed so sick that three doctors had certified that he could not travel except at serious risk to his life. This certificate declared that he suffered from an intermittent pulse, from enfeebled vital faculties, from frequent dizziness, from melancholia, weakness of the stomach, insomnia, shooting pains and serious hernia.[268] The answer the Pope made to this was to order the Inquisitor to send at Galileo's expense a commissary and a doctor out to his villa to see if he were feigning illness; if he were, he was to be sent bound and in chains to Rome at once; if were really too ill to travel, then he was to be sent in chains as soon as he was convalescent and could travel safely.[269] Galileo did not delay after that any longer than he could help, and set out for Rome in January in a litter supplied by the Tuscan Grand Duke.[270] The journey was prolonged by quarantine, but upon his arrival (February 13, 1633), he was welcomed into the palace of Niccolini, the warm-hearted ambassador of the Grand Duke.

Four times was the old man summoned into the presence of the Holy Office, though never when the Pope was presiding. In his first examination held on the 12th of April, he told how he thought he had obeyed the decree of 1616 as his *Dialogo* did not defend the Copernican doctrine but rather confuted it, and that in his desire to do the right, he had personally submitted the book while in manuscript to the censorship of the Master of the Sacred Palace, and had accepted all the changes he and the Florentine Inquisitor had required. He had not mentioned the affair of 1616 because he thought that order did not apply to this book in which he proved the lack of validity and of conclusiveness of the Copernican arguments.[271] With remarkable, in fact unique, consideration, the Holy Office then assigned Galileo to a suite of rooms within the prisons of the Holy Office, allowed him to have his servant with him and to have his meals sent in by the ambassador. On the 30th after his examination, they even assigned as his prison, the Ambassador's palace, out of consideration for his age and ill-health.

In his second appearance (April 30), Galileo declared he had been thinking matters over after re-reading his book (which he had not read for three years), and freely confessed that there were several passages which would mislead a reader unaware of his real intentions, into believing the worse arguments were the better, and he blamed these slips upon his vain ambition and delight in his own skill in debate.[272] He thereupon offered to write another "day" or two more for the *Dialogo* in which he would completely refute the two "strong" Copernican arguments based on the sun's spots and on the tides.[273] Ten days later, at his third appearance, he presented a written statement of his defence in which he claimed that the phrase *vel quovis modo docere* was wholly new to him, and that he had obeyed the order given him by Cardinal Bellarmin over the latter's own signature. However he would make what amends he could and begged the Cardinals to "consider his miserable bodily health and his incessant mental trouble for the past ten months, the discomforts of a long hard journey at the worst season, when 70 years old, together with the loss of the greater part of the year, and that therefore such suffering might be adequate punishment for his faults which they might condone to failing old age. Also he commended to them his honor and reputation against the calumnies of his ill-wishers who seek to detract from his good name."[274] To such a plight was the great man brought! But the end was not yet.

Nearly a month later (June 16), by order of the Pope, Galileo was once again interrogated, this time under threat of torture.[275] Once again he declared the opinion of Ptolemy true and indubitable and said he did not hold and had not held this doctrine of Copernicus after he had been informed of the order to abandon it. "As for the rest," he added, "I am in your hands, do with me as you please." "I am here to obey."[276] Then by the order of the Pope, ensued Galileo's complete abjuration on his knees in the presence of the full Congregation, coupled with his promise to denounce other heretics (i.e., Copernicans).[277] In addition, because he was guilty of the heresy of having held and believed a doctrine declared and defined as contrary to the Scriptures, he was sentenced to "formal imprisonment" at the will of the Congregation, and to repeat the seven penitential Psalms every week for three years.[278]

At Galileo's earnest request, his sentence was commuted almost at once, to imprisonment first in the archiepiscopal palace in Siena (from June 30-December 1), then in his own villa at Arcetri, outside Florence, though under strict orders not to receive visitors but to live in solitude.[279] In the spring his increasing illness occasioned another request for greater liberty in order to have the necessary visits from the doctor; but on March 23, 1634, this was denied him with a stern command from the Pope to refrain from further petitions lest the Sacred Congregation be compelled to recall him to their prisons in Rome.[280]

The rule forbidding visitors seems not to have been rigidly enforced all the time, for Milton visited him, "a prisoner of the Inquisition" in 1638;[281] yet Father Castelli had to write to Rome for permission to visit him to learn his newly invented method of finding longitude at sea.[282] When in Florence on a very brief stay to see his doctor, Galileo had to have the especial consent of the Inquisitor in order to attend mass at Easter. He won approval from the Holy Congregation, however, by refusing to receive some gifts and letters brought him by some German merchants from the Low Countries.[283] He was then totally blind, but he dragged out his existence until January 8, 1642 (the year of Newton's birth), when he died. As the Pope objected to a public funeral for a man sentenced by the Holy Office, he was buried without even an epitaph.[284] The first inscription was made 31 years later, and in 1737, his remains were removed to Santa Croce after the Congregation had first been asked if such action would be unobjectionable.[285]

Pope Urban had no intention of concealing Galileo's abjuration and sentence. Instead, he ordered copies of both to be sent to all inquisitors and papal nuncios that they might notify all their clergy and especially all the professors of mathematics and philosophy within their districts, particularly those at Florence, Padua and Pisa.[286] This was done during the summer and fall of 1633. From Wilna in Poland, Cologne, Paris, Brussels, and Madrid, as well as from all Italy, came the replies of the papal officials stating that the order had been obeyed.[287] He evidently intended to leave no ground for a remark like that of Fromundus about the earlier condemnation.

Galileo was thus brought so low that the famous remark, "Eppur si muove," legend reports him to have made as he rose to his feet after his abjuration, is incredible in itself, even if it had appeared in history earlier than its first publication in 1761.[288] But his discoveries and his fight in defence of the system did much both to strengthen the doctrine itself and to win adherents to it. The appearance of the moon as seen through a telescope destroyed the Aristotelian notion of the perfection of heavenly bodies. Jupiter's satellites gave proof by analogy of the solar system, though on a smaller scale. The discovery of the phases of Venus refuted a hitherto strong objection to the Copernican system; and the discovery of the spots on the sun led to his later discovery of the sun's axial rotation, another proof by analogy of the axial rotation of the earth. Yet he swore the Ptolemaic conception was the true one.

The abjuration of Galileo makes a pitiful page in the history of thought and has been a fruitful source of controversy[289] for nearly three centuries. He was unquestionably a sincere and loyal Catholic, and accordingly submitted to the punishment decreed by the authorities. But in his abjuration he plainly perjured himself, however fully he may be pardoned for it because of the extenuating circumstances. Had he not submitted and been straitly imprisoned, if not burned, the world would indeed have been the poorer by the loss of his greatest work, the *Dialoghi delle Nuove Scienze*, which he did not publish until 1636.[290]

Even more hotly debated has been the action of the Congregations in condemning the Copernican doctrine, and sentencing Galileo as a heretic for upholding it.[291] Though both Paul V and Urban VIII spurred on these actions, neither signed either the decree or the sentence, nor was the latter present at Galileo's examinations. Pope Urban would prefer not so openly to have changed his position from that of tolerance to his present one of active opposition caused partly by his piqued self-respect[292] and partly by his belief that this heresy was more dangerous even than that of Luther and Calvin.[293] It is a much mooted question whether the infallibility of the Church was involved or not. Though the issue at stake was not one of faith, nor were the decrees issued by the Pope *ex cathedra*, but by a group of Cardinals, a fallible body, yet they had the full approbation of the Popes, and later were published in the Index preceded by a papal bull excommunicating those who did not obey the decrees contained therein.[294] It seems to be a matter of the letter as opposed to the spirit of the law. De Morgan points out that contemporary opinion as represented by Fromundus, an ardent opponent of Galileo, did not consider the Decree of the Index or of the Inquisition as a declaration of the Church,[295] — a position which Galileo himself may have held, thus explaining his practical disregard of the decree of 1616 after he was persuaded the authorities were more favorably disposed to him. But M. Martin, himself a Catholic, thinks[296] that theoretically the Congregations could punish Galileo only for disobedience of the secret order, — but even so his book had been examined and passed by the official censors.

When the Index was revised under Pope Benedict XIV in 1757, largely through the influence of the Jesuit astronomer Boscovich, so it is said,[297] the phrase prohibiting all books teaching the immobility of the sun, and the mobility of the earth was omitted from the decrees.[298] But in 1820, the Master of the Sacred Palace refused to permit the publication in Rome of a textbook on astronomy by Canon Settele, who thereupon appealed to the Congregations. They granted his request in August, and two years later, issued a decree approved by Pope Pius VII ordering the Master of the Sacred Palace in future "not to refuse license for publication of books dealing with the mobility of the earth and the immobility of the sun according to the common opinion of modern astronomers" on that ground alone.[299] The next edition of the *Index Librorum Prohibitorum* (1835) did not contain the works of Copernicus, Galileo, Foscarini, à Stunica and Kepler which had appeared in every edition up to that time since their condemnation in 1616, (Kepler's in 1619).

# CHAPTER III.
## THE OPPOSITION AND THEIR ARGUMENTS.

THE Protestant leaders had rejected the Copernican doctrine as contrary to the Scriptures. The Roman Congregations had now condemned Galileo for upholding this doctrine after they had prohibited it for the same reasons. These objections are perhaps best summarized in that open letter Foscarini wrote to the general of his order, the Carmelites, at Naples in January, 1615,[300] — the letter that was absolutely prohibited by the Index in March, 1616. He gave these arguments and answered them lest, as he said, "whilst otherwise the opinion is favored with much probability, it be found in reality to be extremely repugnant (as at first sight it seems) not only to physical reasons and common principles received on all hands (which cannot do so much harm), but also (which would be of far worse consequence) to many authorities of Sacred Scripture. Upon which account many at first looking into it explode it as the most fond paradox and monstrous *capriccio* that ever was heard of." "Yet many modern authors," he says further on, "are induced to follow it, but with much hesitancy and fear, in regard that it seemeth in their opinion so to contradict the Holy Scriptures that it cannot possibly be reconciled to them." Consequently Foscarini argued that the theory is either true or false; if false, it ought not to be divulged; if true, the authority of the Sacred Scriptures will not oppose it; neither does one truth contradict another. So he turned to the Bible.

He found that six groups of authorities seemed to oppose this doctrine. (1) Those stating that the earth stands fast, as Eccles. 1:4. (2) Those stating that the sun moves and revolves; as Psalm XIX, Isaiah XXXVIII, and the miracle in Josh. X:12-14. (3) Those speaking of the heaven above and the earth beneath, as in Joel II. Also Christ came *down* from Heaven. (4) Those authorities who place Hell at the center of the world, a "common opinion of divines," because it ought to be in the lowest part of the world, that is, at the center of the sphere. Then by the Copernican hypothesis, Hell must either be in the sun; or, if in the earth, if the earth should move about the sun, then Hell within the earth would be in Heaven, and nothing could be more absurd. (5) Those authorities opposing Heaven to earth and earth to Heaven, as in Gen. I, Mat.

VI, etc. Since the two are always mutually opposed to each other, and Heaven undoubtedly refers to the circumference, earth must necessarily be at the center. (6) Those authorities ("rather of fathers and divines than of the Sacred Scriptures") who declare that after the Day of Judgment, the sun shall stand immovable in the east and the moon in west.

Foscarini then lays down in answer six maxims, the first of which is that things attributed to God must be expounded metaphorically according to our manner of understanding and of common speech. The other maxims are more metaphysical, as that everything in the universe, whether corruptible or incorruptible, obeys a fixed law of its nature; so, for example, Fortune is *always* fickle. In concluding his defense, he claims among other things, that the Copernician is a more admirable hypothesis than the Ptolemaic, and that it is an easy way into astronomy and philosophy. Then he adds that there may be an analogy between the seven-branched candlestick of the Old Testament and the seven planets around the sun, and possibly the arrangement of the seeds in the "Indian Figg," in the pomegranate and in grapes is all divine evidence of the solar system. With such an amusing reversion to mediæval analogy his spirited letter ends.

Some or all of these scriptural arguments appear in most of the attacks on the doctrine even before its condemnation by the Index in 1616 was widely known. Besides these objections, Aristotle's and Ptolemy's statements were endlessly repeated with implicit faith in their accuracy. Even Sir Francis Bacon (1567-1631) with all his modernity of thought, failed in this instance to recognize the value of the new idea and, despite his interest in Galileo's discoveries, harked back to the time-honored objections. At first mild in his opposition, he later became emphatically opposed to it. In the *Advancement of Learning* [301] (1604), he speaks of it as a possible explanation of the celestial phenomena according to astronomy but as contrary to natural philosophy. Some fifteen years later in the *Novum Organon*,[302] he asserts that the assumption of the earth's movement cannot be allowed; for, as he says in his *Thema Cœli*,[303] at that time he considered the opinion that the earth is stationary the truer one. Finally, in his *De Augmentis Scientiarum* [304] (1622-1623) he speaks of the old notions of the solidity of the heavens, etc., and adds, "It is the absurdity of these opinions that has driven men to the diurnal motion; which I am convinced is most false." He gives his reasons in the *Descriptio Globi Intellectualis* [305] (ch. 5-6): "In favor of the earth [as the center of the world] we have the evidence of our sight, and an inveterate opinion; and most of all this, that as dense bodies are contracted into a narrow compass, and rare bodies are widely diffused (and the area of every circle is contracted to the center) it seems to follow almost of necessity that the narrow space about the middle of the world be set down as the proper and peculiar place for dense bodies." The sun's claims to such a situation are satisfied through having two satellites of its own, Venus and Mercury. Copernicus's scheme is inconvenient; it overloads the earth with a triple motion; it creates a difficulty by separating the sun from the number of the planets with which it has much in common; and the "introduction of so much immobility into nature ... and making the moon revolve around the earth in an epicycle, and some other assumptions of his are the speculations of one who cares not what fictions he introduces into nature, provided his calculations answer." The total absence of all reference to the Scriptures is the unique and refreshing part of Bacon's thought.

All the more common arguments against the diurnal rotation of the earth are well stated in an interesting little letter (1619) by Thomas Feyens, or Fienus, a professor at the school of medicine in the University of Louvain. [306] Thus Catholic, Protestant, and unbeliever, Feyens, Melancthon, Bacon and Bodin, all had recourse to the same arguments to oppose this seemingly absurd doctrine.

Froidmont, or Fromundus, the good friend and colleague of Feyens at Louvain, was also much interested in these matters, so much so that some thought he had formerly accepted the Copernican doctrine and "only fled back into the camp of Aristotle and Ptolemy through terror at the decree of the S. Congregation of Cardinals."[307] His indignant denial of this imputation of turn-coat in 1634 is somewhat weakened by reference to his *Saturnalitæ Coenæ* [308] (1615) in which he suggests that, if the Copernican doctrine is admitted, then Hell may be in the sun at the center of the universe rather than in the earth, in order to be as far as possible from Paradise. He also refers in his *De Cometa* (1618) to the remark of Justus-Lipsius[309] that this paradox was buried with Copernicus, saying "You are mistaken, O noble scholar: it lives, and it is full of vigor even now among many,"[310] thus apparently not seeing serious objection to it. M. Monchamp summarizes Froidmont's point of view as against Aristotle and Ptolemy, half for Copernicus and wholly for Tycho Brahe.

Froidmont's best known books are the two he wrote in answer to a defense of the Copernican position first by Philip Lansberg, then by his son. The *Ant-Aristarchus sive Orbis Terræ Immobilis, Liber unicus in quo decretum S. Congregationis S.R.E. Cardinal. an. 1616, adversus Pythagorico-Copernicanus editum, defenditur*, appeared in 1631 before Galileo's condemnation. The Jesuit Cavalieri wrote to Galileo in May about it thus:[311] "I have run it through, and verily it states the Copernican theory and the arguments in its favor with so much skill and efficacy that he seems to have understood it very well indeed. But he refutes them with so little force that he seems rather to be of an opinion contrary to that expressed in the title of his book. I have given it to M. César. If you wish it, I will have it sent to you. The arguments he brings against Copernicus are those you have so masterfully stated and answered in your *Dialogo.*" Nearly a year later, Galileo wrote to Gassendi and Diodati that he had received this book a month before and, although he had been unable to read much of it on account of his eye trouble, it seemed to him that of all the opponents of Copernicus whom he had seen, Fromundus was the most sensible and efficient.[312] Again he wrote in January, 1633, regretting that he had not seen it till six months after he had published his dialogues, for he would have both praised it and commented upon certain points. "As for Fromundus (who however shows himself to be a man of great talent) I wish he had not fallen into what seems to me a truly serious error, although a rather common one, in order to refute the Copernican opinion, of beginning by poking scorn and ridicule at those who consider it true, and then (what seems to me still less becoming) of basing his attack chiefly on the authority of the Scriptures, and finally of deducing from this that in this respect it is an opinion little short of heretical. To argue in this way is clearly not praiseworthy;" for as Galileo goes on to show, if the Scriptures are the word of God, the heavens themselves are his handiwork. Why is the one less noble than the other?[313]

Froidmont replied in 1633 to Lansberg's reply with his second attack, *Vesta, sive Ant-Aristarchi Vindex*, in which he laid even more emphasis upon the theological and scriptural objections. Yet, in ignorance of Galileo's condemnation, he considers the charge of heresy too strong. "The partisans of this system do not after all disdain the authority of the Scriptures, although they appear to interpret it in a way rather in their favor." He also, and rightly, denies the existence at that time of any conclusive proof.[314]

In spite of Froidmont's position, the University of Louvain was not cordial in its response to the papal nuncio's announcement in September, 1633, of Galileo's abjuration and sentence, in marked contrast to the reply sent by the neighboring university of Douay. The latter body, in a letter signed by Matthæus Kellison (Sept. 7, 1633), declared the condemned theory "should be discarded and hissed from the schools; and that in the English College there in Douay, this paradox never had been approved and never would be, but had always been opposed and always would be."[315]

This opposition in the universities in Belgium continued throughout the century to be based not so much on scientific grounds as upon the Bible. This may be seen in the manuscript reports of lectures in physics and astronomy given at Liège in 1662, and at Louvain between 1650-1660, though one of these does not mention the decree of 1616.[316] The general congregation of the Society of Jesus in 1650 drew up a list of the propositions proscribed in their teaching, though, according to M. Monchamp (himself a Catholic) not thereby implying a denial of any probability they might have. The 35th proposition ran: "Terra movetur motu diurno; planetæ, tanquam viventia, moventur ab intrinseco. Firmamentum stat."[317] The Jesuit astronomer Tacquet in his textbook (Antwerp, 1669) respected this decision, acknowledging that no scientific reason kept him from defending the theory, but solely his respect for the Christian faith.[318]

One of the pupils of the Jesuits revolted however. Martin van Welden, appointed professor of mathematics at Louvain in 1683, debated a series of theses in January, 1691. The second read: "Indubitum est systhema Copernici de planetarum motu circa sole; inter quos merito terra censetur." His refusal to alter the wording except to change *indubitum* to *certum* brought on a stormy controversy within the faculty which eventually reached the Council of Brabant and the papal nuncio at Brussels.[319] The professor finally submitted, though he was not forbidden to teach the Copernician system, nor did the faculty affirm its falsity, merely that it was contrary to the Roman decree. The professor re-opened the matter with a similar thesis in July, thereby arousing a second controversy that this time reached even the Privy Council. Once more he submitted, but solely with an apology for having caused a disagreement. His new theses in 1695 contained no explicit mention of the Copernician system; at least he had learned tact.[320]

The absorption of the German states in the Thirty Years War may account for the apparent absence there of Copernican discussion until after the Peace of Westphalia. A certain Georgius Ludovicus Agricola gave a syllogistic refutation of the doctrine as his disputation at the university of Wittenberg in 1665. While he acknowledged its ingenuity, he preferred to it "the noblest, truest, and divinely inspired system" of Tycho Brahe. The four requirements of an acceptable astronomical hypothesis according to this student are: (1) That it suit all the observations of all the ages; (2) That as far as possible, it be simple and clear; (3) That it be not contrary to the principles of physics and optics; (4) That it be not contrary to the Holy Scriptures. As the Copernican theory does not meet all these tests, it is unsatisfactory. Incidentally, he considers it "ridiculous to include the earth among the planets, because then we would be living in Heaven, forsooth, since we would be in a star." He decides finally "that the decree of March, 1616, condemning the Copernican opinion was not unjust, nor was Galileo unfairly treated."[321]

Two years later appeared a textbook at Nürnberg, by a Jesuit father, based on the twelfth century Sacrobosco treatise and without a single reference so far as I could find, to Copernicus![322] Another publication of the same year was a good deal more up to date. This was a kind of catechism in German by Johann-Henrich Voight[323] explaining for the common people various scientific and mathematical problems in a hundred questions and answers.

He himself, a Royal Swedish astronomer, obviously preferred the Tychonic system, but he left his reader free to choose between that and the Copernican one, both of which he carefully explained.[324] He made an interesting summary in parallel columns of the arguments for and against the earth's motion which it seems worth while to repeat as an instance of what the common people were taught:

| Reasons for asserting the earth is motionless: | Reasons for the belief that the earth is moved: |
|---|---|
| 1. David in Psalm 89: God has founded the earth and it shall not be moved. | 1. The sun, the most excellent, the greatest and the midmost star, rightly stands still like a king while all the other stars with the earth swing round it. |
| 2. Joshua bade the sun stand still—which would not be notable were it not already at rest. | 2. That you believe that the heavens revolve is due to ocular deception similar to that of a man on a ship leaving shore. |
| 3. The earth is the heaviest element, therefore it more probably is at rest. | 3. That Joshua bade the sun stand still Moses wrote for the people in accordance with the popular misconception. |
| 4. Everything loose on the earth seeks its rest on the earth, why should not the whole earth itself be at rest? | 4. As the planets are each a special created thing in the heavens, so the earth is a similar creation and similarly revolves. |
| 5. We always see half of the heavens and the fixed stars also in a great half circle, which we could not see if the earth moved, and especially if it declined to the north and south.... | 5. The sun fitly rests at the center as the heart does in the middle of the human body. |
| 6. A stone or an arrow shot straight up falls straight down. But if the earth turned under it, from west to east, it must fall west of its starting point. | 6. Since the earth has in itself its especial centrum, a stone or an arrow falls freely out of the air again to its own centrum as do all earthly things. |
| 7. In such revolutions houses and towers would fall in heaps. | 7. The earth can move five miles in a second more readily than the sun can go forty miles in the same time. |
| 8. High and low tide could not exist; the flying of birds and the swimming of fish would be hindered and all would be in a state of dizziness. | |

And similarly on both sides.[325]

Another writer preferring the Tychonic scheme was Longomontanus, whose *Astronomica Danica* (Amsterdam, 1640) upheld this theory because it "obviates the absurdities of the Copernican hypothesis and most aptly corresponds to celestial appearances," and also because it is "midway between that and the Ptolemaic one."[326] Even though he speaks of the "apparent motion of the sun," he attributed diurnal motion to the heavens, and believed the earth was at the center of the universe because (1), from the account of the Creation, the heaven and the earth were first created, and what could be more likely than that the heavens should fill the space between the center (the earth) and the circumference? (2) and because of the incredibly enormous interval between the sphere of the fixed stars and the earth necessitated by Copernican doctrine.[327]

The high-water mark of opposition after Galileo's condemnation was reached in the *Almagestum Novum* (Bologna, 1651) by Father Riccioli of the Society of Jesus. It was the authoritative answer of that order, the leaders of the Church in matters of education, to the challenges of the literary world for a justification of the condemnation of the Copernican doctrine and of Galileo for upholding it. Father Riccioli had been professor of philosophy and of mathematics for six years and of theology for ten when by order of his superiors, he was released from his lectureship to prepare a book containing all the material he could gather together on this great controversy of the age. [328] He wrote it as he himself said, as "an *apologia* for the Sacred Congregation of the Cardinals who officially pronounced these condemnations, not so much because I thought such great height and eminence needed this at my hands but especially in behalf of Catholics; also out of the love of truth to which every non-Catholic, even, should be persuaded and from a certain notable zeal and eagerness for the preservation of the Sacred Scriptures intact and unimpaired; and lastly because of that reverence and devotion which I owe from my particular position toward the Holy, Catholic and Apostolic Church."[329]

This monumental work, the most important literary production of the Society in the 17th century,[330] is abundant witness to Riccioli's remarkable erudition and industry. Nearly one-fifth of the total bulk of the two huge volumes is devoted to a statement of the Copernican controversy. This is prefaced by a brief account of his own theory of the universe—the invention of which is another proof of the ability of the man—for his scientific training prevented his acceptance of the Aristotelian-Ptolemaic theory in the light of Galileo's discoveries; his position as a Jesuit and a faithful son of the Church precluded him from adopting the system condemned by its representatives; and Tycho Brahe's scheme was not wholly to his liking. Therefor he proposed an adaptation of the last-named, more in accordance, as he thought, with the facts.[331] Where Tycho had all the planets except the earth and the moon encircle the sun, and that in turn, together with the moon and the sphere of the fixed stars, sweep around the earth as the center of the universe, Riccioli made only Mars, Mercury and Venus encircle the sun, — Mars with an orbit the radius of which included the earth within its sweep, the other two planets with orbital radii shorter than that of the sun, and so excluding the earth. This he did, (1) because both Jupiter and Saturn have their own kingdoms in the heavens, and Mars, Mercury and Venus are but satellites of the sun; (2) because there are greater varieties of eccentricity among these three than the other two; (3) because Saturn and Jupiter are the greatest planets and with the sphere of the fixed stars move more slowly; (4) Mars belongs with the sun because of their related movements; and (5) because it is likely that one of the planets would have much in common both with Saturn and Jupiter and with Mercury and Venus also.[332]

Then he takes up the attack upon the Copernican doctrine. M. Delambre summarizes and comments upon 57 of his arguments against it,[333] and Riccioli himself claims[334] to have stated "40 new arguments in behalf of Copernicus and 77 against him." But these sound somewhat familiar to the reader of anti-Copernican literature: as, for instance, "which is more natural, straight or circular movement?" Or, the Copernican argument that movement is easier if the object moved is smaller involves a matter of Faith since it implies a question of God's power; for to God all is alike, there is no hard nor easy.[335] Although diurnal movement is useful to the earth alone and so, according to the Copernicans, the earth should have the labor of it, Riccioli argues that everything was created for man; let the stars revolve around him. The sun may be nobler than the earth, but man is nobler than the sun.[336] If the earth's movement were admitted, Ptolemy's defense would be broken down through the elimination of the epicycles of the superior planets: here, if ever, the Copernicans appear to score, as Riccioli himself admits,[337] but he calls to his aid Tycho Brahe and the Bible. "To invoke such aids is to avow his defeat" is M. Delambre's comment at this point.[338] There are many more arguments, of which the foregoing are but instances chosen more or less at random; but no one of them is of especial weight or novelty.

To strengthen his case, Riccioli listed the supporters of the heliocentric doctrine throughout the ages, with those of the opposite view. If a man's fame adds to the weight of his opinion, the modern reader will be inclined to think the Copernicans have the best of it, for omitting the ancients, most of those opposing it are obscure men.[339]

| In favor of the Copernican doctrine [references omitted].[340] | Against the hypothesis of the earth's movement. |
| --- | --- |
| | Aristotle |
| | Ptolemy |
| | Theon the Alexandrine |
| | Regiomontanus |
| | Alfraganus |
| | Macrobius |
| | Cleomedes |
| | Petrus Aliacensis |
| | George Buchanan |
| | Maurolycus |
| Copernicus | Clavius |
| Rheticus | Barocius |
| Mæstlin | Michael Neander |
| Kepler | Telesius |
| Rothman | Martinengus |
| Galileo | Justus-Lipsius |
| Gilbert (diurnal motion) | Scheiner |
| Foscarini | Tycho |
| Didacus Stunica (sic) | Tasso |
| Ismael Bullialdus | Scipio Claramontius |
| Jacob Lansberg | Michael Incofer |
| Peter Herigonus | Fromundus |
| Gassendi, — "but submits his intellect captive to the Church decrees." | Jacob Ascarisius |
| | Julius Cæsar La Galla |
| Descartes "inclines to this belief." | Tanner |
| A.L. Politianus | Bartholomæus Amicus |
| Bruno | Antonio Rocce |
| | Marinus Mersennius |
| | Polacco |
| | Kircher |
| | Spinella |
| | Pineda |
| | Lorinis |
| | Mastrius |
| | Bellutris |
| | Poncius |
| | Delphinus |
| | Elephantutius |

Riccioli nevertheless viewed the Copernican system with much sympathy. After a full statement of it, he comments: "We have not yet exhausted the full profundities of the Copernican hypothesis, for the deeper one digs into it, the more ingenious and valuable subtilties may one unearth." Then he adds that "the greatness of Copernicus has never been sufficiently appreciated nor will it be, — that man who accomplished what no astronomer before him had scarcely been able even to suggest without an insane machinery of spheres, for by a triple motion of the earth he abolished epicycles and eccentrics. What before so many Atlases could not support, this one Hercules has dared to carry. Would that he had kept himself within the limits of his hypothesis!"[341]

His conclusions seem to show that only his position as a Jesuit restrained him from being a Copernican himself.[342] "I. If the celestial phenomena alone are considered, they are equally well explained by the two hypotheses [Ptolemaic and Copernican]. II. The physical evidence as explained in the two systems with exception of percussion and the speed of bodies driven north or south, and east or west, is all for immobility. III. One might waver indifferently between the two hypotheses aside from the witness of the Scriptures, which settles the question. IV. There are in addition plenty of other motives besides Scriptural ones for rejecting this system." (!) But with the Scriptural evidence he adduces the decree of the Index under Paul V against the doctrine, and the sentence of Galileo, so that "the sole possible conclusion is that the earth stands by nature immobile in the center of the universe, and the sun moves around it with both a diurnal and an annual motion."[343]

Even this great book was as insufficient to stop the criticism of the action of the Congregations, as it was to stop the spread of the doctrine. So once again the father took up the cudgels in defense of the Church. The full title of his *Apologia* runs: "An Apologia in behalf of an argument from physical mathematics against the Copernican system, directed against that system by a new argument from the reflex motion of falling weights." (Venice, 1669). He states in this that his *Almagestum Novum* had received the approbation of professors of mathematics at Bologna, of one at Pisa, and of another at Padua, and he quotes the conclusion from *Nicetas Orthodoxus* ("a diatribe by Julius Turrinus, doctor of mathematics, philosophy, medicine, law, and Greek letters"): "That the sun is revolved by diurnal and by annual motion, and that the earth is at rest I firmly hold, infallibly believe, and openly confess, not because of mathematical reasons, but solely at the command of faith, by the authority of the Scriptures, and the nod of approval (*nutu*) of the Roman See, whose rules laid down at the dictation of the spirit of truth, may I, as befits everyone, uphold as law."[344]

Riccioli further on proceeds to answer his objecters, declaring that "the Church did not decide *ex cathedra* that the Scripture concerning movement should be interpreted literally; that the censure was laid by qualified theologians and approved by eminent cardinals, and was not merely provisional, nor for the time being absolute, since the contrary could never be demonstrated; and that while it was the primary intent of the Inquisitors to condemn the opinion as heretical and directly contrary to the Scriptures ... they added that it was absurd and false also in philosophy, in order, not to avert any objections which could be on the side of philosophy or astronomy, but only lest any one should say that Scripture is opposed to philosophy."[345] These answers are indicative of the type of criticism with which the Church had to cope even at that time.[346]

# CHAPTER IV.
## THE GRADUAL ACCEPTANCE OF THE COPERNICAN SYSTEM.

JUST as Tycho Brahe's system proved to be for some a good half-way station between the improbable Ptolemaic and the heretical Copernican system;[347] so the Cartesian philosophy helped others to reconcile their scientific knowledge with their reverence for the Scriptures, until Newton's work had more fully demonstrated the scientific truth.

Its originator, Réné Descartes[348] (1596-1650) was in Holland when word of Galileo's condemnation reached him in 1633, as he was seeking in the bookshops of Amsterdam and Leyden for a copy of the *Dialogo*.[349] He at once became alarmed lest he too be accused of trying to establish the movement of the earth, a doctrine which he had understood was then publicly taught even in Rome, and which he had made the basis of his own philosophy. If this doctrine were condemned as false, then his philosophy must be also; and, true to his training by the Jesuits, rather than go against the Church he would not publish his books. He set aside his *Cosmos*, and delayed the publication of the *Méthode* for some years in consequence, even starting to translate it into Latin as a safeguard.[350] His conception of the universe, the Copernican one modified to meet the requirements of a literally interpreted Bible, was not printed until 1644, when it appeared in his *Principes*.[351]

According to this statement which he made only as a possible explanation of the phenomena and not as an absolute truth, while there was little to choose between the Tychonic and the Copernican conceptions, he inclined slightly toward the former. He conceived of the earth and the other planets as each borne along in its enveloping heaven like a ship by the tide, or like a man asleep on a ship that was sailing from Calais to Dover. The earth itself does not move, but it is transported so that its position is changed in relation to the other planets but not visibly so in relation to the fixed stars because of the vast intervening spaces. The laws of the universe affect even the most minute particle, and all alike are swept along in a series of vortices, or whirlpools, of greater or less size. Thus the whole planetary system sweeps around the sun in one great vortex, as the satellites sweep around their respective planets in lesser ones. In this way Descartes worked out a mechanical explanation of the universe of considerable importance because it was a rational one which anyone could understand. Its defects were many, to be sure, as for example, that it did not allow for the elliptical orbits of the planets;[352] and one critic has claimed that this theory of a motionless earth borne along by an enveloping heaven was comparable to a worm in a Dutch cheese sent from Amsterdam to Batavia, – the worm has travelled about 6000 leagues but without changing its place![353] But this theory fulfilled Descartes's aim: to show that the universe was governed by mechanical laws of which we can be absolutely certain and that Galileo's discoveries simply indicated this.[354]

This exposition of the Copernican doctrine strongly appealed to the literary world of the 17th and 18th centuries in western Europe, especially in the Netherlands, in the Paris salons and in the universities.[355] M. Monchamp cites a number of contemporary comments upon its spread, in one of which it is claimed that in 1691, the university of Louvain had for the preceding forty years been practically composed of Cartesians.[356] For the time being, this theory was a more or less satisfactory explanation of the universe according to known laws; it answered to Galileo's observations; it was in harmony with the Scriptures, and its vortices paved the way for the popular acceptance of Newton's law of universal gravitation.

Protestant England was of course little disturbed by the decree against the Copernican doctrine, a fact that makes it possible, perhaps, to see there more clearly the change in people's attitude from antagonism to acceptance, than in Catholic Europe where fear of the Church's power, and respect for its decisions inhibited honest public expression of thought and conviction. While in England also the literal interpretation of the Scriptures continued to be with the common people a strong objection against the doctrine, the rationalist movement of the late seventeenth and eighteenth centuries along with Newton's great work, helped win acceptance for it among the better educated classes.

Bruno had failed to win over his English hearers, and in 1600 when the *De Magnete* was published, William Gilbert, (1540-1603) was apparently the only supporter of the earth's movement then in England,[357] and he advocated the diurnal motion only.[358] Not many, however, were as outspoken as Bacon in denunciation of the system; they were simply somewhat ironically indifferent. An exception to this was Dean Wren of Windsor (father of the famous architect). He could not speak strongly enough against it in his marginal notes on Browne's *Pseudodoxia Epidemica*. As Dr. Johnson wrote,[359] Sir Thomas Browne (1605-1682) himself in his zeal for the old errors, did not easily admit new positions, for he never mentioned the motion of the earth but with contempt and ridicule. This was not enough for the Dean, who wrote in the margin of Browne's book, at such a passage,[360] that there were "eighty-odd expresse places in the Bible affirming in plaine and overt terms the naturall and perpetuall motion of sun and moon" and that "a man should be affrighted to follow that audacious and pernicious suggestion which Satan used, and thereby undid us all in our first parents, that God hath a double meaning in his commands, in effect condemning God of amphibologye. And all this boldness and overweaning having no other ground but a seeming argument of some phenomena forsooth, which notwithstanding we know the learned Tycho, prince of astronomers, who lived fifty-two years since Copernicus, hath by admirable and matchlesse instruments and many yeares exact observations proved to bee noe better than a dreame."

Richard Burton (1576-1639) in *The Anatomy of Melancholy* speaks of the doctrine as a "prodigious tenent, or paradox," lately revived by "Copernicus, Brunus and some others," and calls Copernicus in consequence the successor of Atlas.[361] The vast extent of the heavens that this supposition requires, he considers "quite opposite to reason, to natural philosophy, and all out as absurd as disproportional, (so some will) as prodigious, as that of the sun's swift motion of the heavens." If the earth is a planet, then other planets may be inhabited (as Christian Huygens argued later on); and this involves a possible plurality of worlds. Burton laughs at those who, to avoid the Church attitude and yet explain the celestial phenomena, invent new hypotheses and new systems of the world, "correcting others, doing worse themselves, reforming some and marring all," as he says of Roeslin's endeavors. "In the meantime the world is tossed in a blanket amongst them; they hoyse the earth up and down like a ball, make it stand and goe at their pleasure."[362] He himself was indifferent.

Others more sensitive to the implications of this system, might exclaim with George Herbert (1593-1633):[363]

"Although there were some fourtie heav'ns, or more,
Sometimes I peere above them all;
Sometimes I hardly reach a score,
Sometimes to hell I fall.

"O rack me not to such a vast extent,
Those distances belong to thee.
The world's too little for thy tent,
A grave too big for me."

Or they might waver, undecided, like Milton who had the archangel answer Adam's questions thus:[364]

"But whether thus these things, or whether not,
Whether the Sun predominant in Heaven
Rise on the Earth, or Earth rise on the Sun,
Hee from the East his flaming robe begin,
Or Shee from West her silent course advance
With inoffensive pace that spinning sleeps
On her soft axle, while she paces ev'n
And bears thee soft with the smooth Air along,
Solicit not thy thoughts with matters hid,
Leave them to God above, him serve and feare;
Of other Creatures, as him pleases best,
Wherever plac't, let him dispose; joy thou
In what he gives to thee, this Paradise
And the fair Eve: Heaven is for thee too high
To know what passes there: be lowlie wise." (1667)

Whewell thinks[365] that at this time the diffusion of the Copernican system was due more to the writings of Bishop Wilkins than to those of any one else, for their very extravagances drew stronger attention to it. The first, "The Discovery of a New World: or a Discourse tending to prove that there may be another habitable world in the moon," appeared in 1638; and a third edition was issued only two years later together with the second book; "Discourse concerning a New Planet — that 'tis probable our Earth is one of the planets." In this latter, the Bishop stated certain propositions as indubitable; among these were, that the scriptural passages intimating diurnal motion of the sun or of the heavens are fairly capable of another interpretation; that there is no sufficient reason to prove the earth incapable of those motions which Copernicus ascribes to it; that it is more probable the earth does move than the heavens, and that this hypothesis is exactly agreeable to common appearances.[366] And these books appeared when political and constitutional matters, and not astronomical ones, were the burning questions of the day in England.

The spread of the doctrine was also helped by Thomas Salusbury's translations of the books and passages condemned by the Index in 1616 and 1619. This collection, "intended for gentlemen," he published by popular subscription immediately after the Restoration,[367] a fact that indicates that not merely mathematicians (whom Whewell claims[368] were by that time all decided Copernicans) but the general public were interested and awake.[369]

The appearance of Newton's *Principia* in 1687 with his statement of the universal application of the law of gravitation, soon ended hesitancy for most people. Twelve years later, John Keill, (1671-1721), the Scotch mathematician and astronomer at Oxford, refuted Descartes's theory of vortices and opened the first course of lectures delivered at Oxford on the new Newtonian philosophy.[370] Not only were his lectures thronged, but his books advocating the Copernican system in full[371] went through several editions in relatively few years.

In the Colonies, Yale University which had hitherto been using Gassendi's textbook, adopted the Newtonian ideas a few years later, partly through the gift to the university of some books by Sir Isaac himself, and partly through the enthusiasm of two young instructors there, Johnson and Brown, who in 1714-1722 widened the mathematical course by including the new theories.[372] The text they used was by Rohault, a Cartesian, edited by Samuel Clarke with critical notes exposing the fallacies of Cartesianism. This "disguised Newtonian treatise" was used at Yale till 1744. The University of Pennsylvania used this same text book even later.[373]

In 1710 Pope (1688-1744) refers to "our Copernican system,"[374] and Addison (1671-1719) in the *Spectator* (July 2, 1711) writes this very modern passage:

> "But among this set of writers, there are none who more gratify and enlarge the imagination, than the authors of the new philosophy, whether we consider their theories of the earth or heavens, the discoveries they have made by glasses, or any other of their contemplations on nature.... But when we survey the whole earth at once, and the several planets that lie within its neighborhood, we are filled with a pleasing astonishment, to see so many worlds hanging one above another, and sliding around their axles in such an amazing pomp and solemnity. If, after this, we contemplate those wide fields of æther, that reach in height as far as from Saturn to the fixed stars, and run abroad almost to an infinitude, our imagination finds its capacity filled with so immense a prospect, as puts it upon the stretch to comprehend it. But if we yet rise higher, and consider the fixed stars as so many vast oceans of flame, that are each of them attended with a different set of planets, and still discover new firmaments and new lights, that are sunk farther in those unfathomable depths of æther, so as not to be seen by the strongest of our telescopes, we are lost in such a labyrinth of suns and worlds, and confounded with the immensity and magnificence of nature.

> "Nothing is more pleasant to the fancy, than to enlarge itself by degrees, in its contemplation of the various proportions which its several objects bear to each other, when it compares the body of man to the bulk of the whole earth, the earth to the circle it describes round the sun, that circle to the sphere of the fixed stars, the sphere of the fixed stars to the circuit of the whole creation, the whole creation itself to the infinite space that is everywhere diffused around it; ... But if, after all this, we take the least particle of these animal spirits, and consider its capacity wrought into

a world, that shall contain within those narrow dimensions a heaven and earth, stars and planets, and every different species of living creatures, in the same analogy and proportion they bear to each other in our own universe; such a speculation, by reason of its nicety, appears ridiculous to those who have not turned their thoughts that way, though, at the same time, it is founded on no less than the evidence of a demonstration."[375]

A little later, Cotton Mather declared (1721) that the "Copernican hypothesis is now generally preferred," and "that there is no objection against the motion of the earth but what has had a full solution."[376] Soon the semi-popular scientific books took up the Newtonian astronomy. One such was described as "useful for all sea-faring Men, as well as Gentlemen, and Others."[377] "Newtonianisme pour les Dames" was advertised in France in the forties.[378] By 1738 when Pope wrote the *Universal Prayer*:

"Yet not to earth's contracted span
Thy goodness let me bound
Or think thee Lord alone of man,
When thousand worlds are round,"

the Copernican-Newtonian astronomy had become a commonplace to most well-educated people in England. To be sure, the great John Wesley (1770) considered the systems of the universe merely "ingenious conjectures," but then, he doubted whether "more than Probabilities we shall ever attain in regard to things at so great a distance from us."[379]

The old phraseology, however, did recur occasionally, especially in poetry and in hymns. For instance, a hymnal (preface dated 1806) contains such choice selections as:

"Before the pondr'ous earthly globe
In fluid air was stay'd,
Before the ocean's mighty springs
Their liquid stores display'd" —

and:

"Who led his blest unerring hand
Or lent his needful aid
When on its strong unshaken base
The pondr'ous earth was laid?"[380]

But too much importance should not be attributed to such passages; though poetry and astronomy need not conflict, as Keble illustrated:[381]

"Ye Stars that round the Sun of Righteousness
In glorious order roll...."

By the middle of the 18th century in England, one could say with Horne "that the Newtonian System had been in possession of the chair for some years;"[382] but it had not yet convinced the common people, for as Pike wrote in 1753, "Many Common Christians to this day firmly believe that the earth really stands still and that the sun moves all round the earth once a day: neither can they be easily persuaded out of this opinion, because they look upon themselves bound to believe what the Scripture asserts."[383]

There was, however, just at this time a little group of thinkers who objected to Newton's scheme, "because of the endless uninterrupted flux of matter from the sun in light, an expense which should destroy that orb."[384] These Hutchinsonians conceived of light as pure ether in motion springing forth from the sun, growing more dense the further it goes till it becomes air, and, striking the circumference of the universe (which is perhaps an immovable solid), is thrown back toward the sun and melted into light again. Its force as its tides of motion strike the earth and the other planets produces their constant gyrations.[385] Men like Duncan Forbes, Lord President of the Court of Sessions, and George Horne, President of Magdalen College, Oxford, as a weapon against rationalism, favored this notion that had been expounded by John Hutchinson (1674-1737) in his *Moses's Principia* (1724).[386] They were also strongly attracted by the scriptural symbolism with which the book abounds. Leslie Stephen summarizes their doctrines as (1) extreme dislike for rationalism, (2) a fanatical respect for the letter of the Bible, and (3) an attempt to enlist the rising powers of scientific enquiry upon the side of orthodoxy. [387] This "little eddy of thought"[388] was not of much influence even at that time, but it has a certain interest as indicating the positions men have taken when on the defensive against new ideas.

# CHAPTER V.
# THE CHURCH AND THE NEW ASTRONOMY: CONCLUSION.

ASTRONOMICAL thought on the Continent was more hampered, in the Catholic countries especially, by the restrictive opinions of the Church. Yet in 1757, when the decree prohibiting all books dealing with the Copernican doctrine was removed from the Index, that system had already long been adopted by the more celebrated academies of Europe, for so Mme. de Premontval claimed in 1750; and it was then reaching out to non-scientific readers, through simple accounts for "ladies and others not well versed in these somewhat technical matters."[389] The great landmark in the development of the doctrine was the publication of Newton's *Principia* in 1687, though its effect in Europe was of course slower in being felt than it was in England. Newton's work and that of the astronomers immediately following him was influential except where the Church's prohibitions still held sway.

During this period, the books published in free Holland were more outspoken in their radical acceptance or in their uncertainty of the truth than were those published in the Catholic countries. Christian Huygens's treatises on the plurality of worlds not only fully accepted the Copernican doctrine, but like those of Bishop Wilkins in England, deduced therefrom the probability that the other planets are inhabited even as the earth is. A writer[390] on the sphere in 1697 stated the different theories of the universe so that his readers might choose the one that to them appeared the most probable. He himself preferred the Cartesian explanation as the simplest and most convenient of all, "though it should be held merely as an hypothesis and not as in absolute agreement with the truth." Pierre Bayle[391] also explained the different systems, but appears himself to waver between the Copernican and the Tychonic conceptions. He used, however, the old word "perigee" (nearness to the earth) rather than the Newtonian "perihelion" (nearness to the sun). His objections to the Copernican doctrine have a familiar ring: It is contrary to the evidence of the senses; a stone would not fall back to its starting-place, nor could a bird return to her nest; the earth would not be equidistant from the horizon and the two poles; and lastly it is contrary to the Scriptures. Only a few years later, however, De Maupertius wrote that no one at that day (1744) doubted any longer the motion of the earth around its axis, and he believed with Newton that the laws of gravity applied to the universe as well as to the earth. Then he proceeded to explain the Copernican system which he favored on the ground of its greater probability.[392]

Even in 1750, Mme. de Premontval thought it wiser to publish in Holland her little life of her father, *Le Méchaniste Philosophe*. This Jean Piegeon, she claimed, was the first man in France to make spheres according to the Copernican system. An orphan, he was educated by a priest; then took up carpentry and mechanics. When he tried to make a celestial sphere according to the Ptolemaic system, he became convinced of its falsity because of its complexities. Therefore he plunged into a study of the new system which he adopted. His first Copernican sphere was exhibited before Louis XIV at Versailles in 1706 and was bought by the king and presented to the Académie des Sciences.[393] The second was taken to Canada by one of the royal officials. Public interest in his work was keen; even Peter the Great, who was then in Paris, visited his workroom.[394] M. Piegeon also wrote a book on the Copernican system.[395]

It seems, however, as though M. Piegeon were slightly in advance of his age, or more daring, perhaps, than his contemporaries, for there was almost no outspoken support of the Copernican system at this time in France. Even Cassini of the French Académie des Sciences did not explicitly support it, though he spoke favorably of it and remarked that recent observations had demonstrated the revolutions of each planet around the sun in accordance with that supposition.[396] But the great orator, Bossuet, (1627-1703), clung to the Ptolemaic conception as alone orthodox, and scriptural.[397] Abbé Fénelon (1651-1715) writing on the existence of God, asked: "Who is it who has hung up this motionless ball of the earth; who has placed the foundations for it," and "who has taught the sun to turn ceasely and regularly in spaces where nothing troubles it?"[398] And a writer on the history of the heavens as treated by poets, philosophers and Moses (1739), tells Gassendi, Descartes and many other great thinkers that their ideas of the heavens are proved vain and false by daily experience as well as by the account of Creation; for the most enlightened experience is wholly and completely in accord with the account of Moses. This book was written, the author said, for young people students of philosophy and the humanities, also for teachers.[399]

The Jesuit order, still a power in Europe in the early 18th century, was bound to the support of the traditional view, which led them into some curious positions in connection with the discoveries made in astronomy during this period. Thus the famous Jesuit astronomer Boscovich (1711-1787) published in Rome in 1746 a study of the ellipticity of the orbits of planets which necessitated the use of the Copernican position; he stated he had assumed it as true merely to facilitate his labors. In the second edition (1785) published some years after the removal from the Index of the decree against books teaching the Copernican doctrine (at his instigation, it is claimed),[400] he added a note to this passage asking the reader to remember the time and the place of its former publication.[401] Just at the end of the preceding century, one of the seminary fathers at Liège maintained that were the earth to move, being made up of so many and divers combustible materials, it would soon burst into flames and be reduced to ashes![402]

During the 18th century at Louvain the Copernican doctrine was warmly supported, but as a theory. A MS. of a course given there in 1748 has come down to us, in which the professor, while affirming its hypothetical character, described it as a simple, clear and satisfactory explanation of the phenomena, then answered all the objections made against it by theologians, physicists, and astronomers.[403] A few years earlier, (1728) a Jesuit at Liège, though well acquainted with Newton's work, declared: "For my part I do not doubt the least in the world that the earth is eternally fixed, for God has founded the terrestrial globe, and it will not be shaken."[404] Another priest stated in the first chapter of his astronomy that the sun and the planets daily revolve around the earth; then later on, he explained the Copernican and the Tychonic schemes and the Cartesian theory of motion with evident sympathy.[405] Two others, one a Jesuit in 1682 at Naples,[406] the other in 1741 at Verona, frankly preferred the Tychonic system, and the latter called the system found by "Tommaso Copernico" a mere fancy.[407] Still another priest, evidently well acquainted with Bradley's work, as late as in 1774 declared that there was nothing decisive on either side of the great controversy between the systems. [408] At this time, however, a father was teaching the Copernican system at Liège without differentiating between thesis and hypothesis.[409] And a Jesuit, while he denied (1772) universal gravitation, the earth's movement, and the plurality of inhabited worlds, declared that the Roman Congregation had done wrong in charging these as heretical suggestions. In fact, M. Monchamp, himself a Catholic priest at Louvain, declared that the Newtonian proofs were considered by many in the 18th century virtually to abrogate the condemnation of 1616 and 1633; hence the professors of the seminary at Liège had adopted the Copernican system.[410]

The famous French astronomer Lalande, in Rome in 1757 when the Inquisition first modified its position, tried to persuade the authorities to remove Galileo's book also from the Index; but his efforts were unavailing, because of the sentence declared against its author.[411] In 1820 Canon Settele was not allowed by the Master of the Sacred Palace to publish his textbook because it dealt with the forbidden subject. His appeal to the Congregation itself resulted, as we have seen, in the decree of 1822 removing this as a cause for prohibition. Yet as late as in 1829, when a statue to Copernicus was being unveiled at Warsaw, and a great convocation had met in the church for the celebration of the mass as part of the ceremony, at the last moment the clergy refused in a body to attend a service in honor of a man whose book was on the Index.[412]

Thus the Roman Catholic Church by reason of its organization and of its doctrine requiring obedience to its authority was more conspicuous for its opposition as a body to the Copernican doctrine, even though as individuals many of its members favored the new system. But the Protestant leaders were quite as emphatic in their denunciations, though less influential because of the Protestant idea of the right to individual belief and interpretation. Luther, Melancthon, Calvin, Turrettin,[413] Owen, and Wesley are some of the notable opponents to it. And when the scientific objections had practically disappeared, those who interpreted the Scriptures literally were still troubled and hesitant down to the present day. Not many years ago, people flocked to hear a negro preacher of the South, Brother Jasper, uphold with all his ability that the sun stood still at Joshua's command, and that today "the sun do move!" Far more surprising is this statement in the new *Catholic Encyclopedia* under "Faith," written by an English Dominican:

> "If, now, the will moves the intellect to consider some debatable point—*e.g.*, the Copernican and Ptolemaic theories of the relationship between the sun and the earth—it is clear that the intellect can only assent to one of these views in proportion that it is convinced that the particular view is true. But neither view has, as far as we can know, more than probable truth, hence of itself the intellect can only give in its partial adherence to one of these views, it must always be precluded from absolute assent by the possibility that the other may be right. The fact that men hold more tenaciously to one of these than the arguments warrant can only be due to some extrinsic consideration, *e.g.*, that it is absurd not to hold to what a vast majority of men hold."

In astronomical thought as in many another field, science and reason have had a hard struggle in men's minds to defeat tradition and the weight of verbal inspiration. Within the Roman Catholic Church opposition to this doctrine was officially weakened in 1757, but not completely ended till the publication of the Index in 1835—the first edition since the decrees of 1616 and 1619 which did not contain the works of Copernicus, Galileo, Foscarini, à Stunica and Kepler. Since then, Roman Catholic writers have been particularly active in defending and explaining the positions of the Church in these matters. They have not agreed among themselves as to whether the infallibility of the Church had been involved in these condemnations, nor as to the reasons for them. As one writer has summarized these diverse positions,[414] they first claimed that Galileo was condemned not for upholding a heresy, but for attempting to reconcile these ideas with the Scriptures, — though in fact he was sentenced specifically for heresy. In their next defense they declared Galileo was not condemned for heresy, but for contumacy and want of respect to the Pope.[415] This statement proving untenable, others held that it was the result of a persecution developing out of a quarrel between Aristotelian professors and those professors who favored experiment, — a still worse argument for the Church itself. Then some claimed that the condemnation was merely provisional, — a position hardly warranted by the wording of the decrees themselves and flatly contradicted by Father Riccioli, the spokesman of the Jesuit authorities.[416] More recently, Roman Catholics have held that Galileo was no more a victim of the Roman Church than of the Protestant — which fails to remove the blame of either. The most recent position is that the condemnation of the doctrine by the popes was not as popes but as men simply, and the Church was not committed to their decision since the popes had not signed the decrees. But two noted English Catholics, Roberts and Mivart, publicly stated in 1870 that the infallibility of the papacy was fully committed in these condemnations by what they termed incontrovertible evidence.[417]

One present-day Catholic calls the action of the Congregations "a theoretical mistake;"[418] another admits it was a deplorable mistake, but practically their only serious one;[419] and a third considers it "providential" since it proved conclusively "that whenever there is apparent contradiction between the truths of science and the truths of faith, either the scientist is declaring as proved what in reality is a mere hypothesis, or the theologian is putting forth his own personal views instead of the teaching of the Gospel."[420] Few would accept today, however, the opinion of the anonymous writer in the *Dublin Review* in the forties that "to the Pontiffs and dignitaries of Rome we are mainly indebted for the Copernican system" and that the phrases "heretical" and "heresy" in the sentence of 1633 were but the *stylus curiæ*, for it was termed heresy only in the technical sense.[421]

The majority of Protestants, with the possible exception of the Lutherans, were satisfied with the probable truth of the Copernican doctrine before the end of the 18th century. Down to the present day, however, there have been isolated protests raised against it, usually on technical grounds supported by reference to the Scriptures. De Morgan refers to one such, "An Inquiry into the Copernican System ... wherein it is proved in the clearest manner, that the earth has only her diurnal motion ... with an attempt to point out the only true way whereby mankind can receive any real benefit from the study of the heavenly bodies, by John Cunningham, London, 1789." De Morgan adds that "the true way appears to be the treatment of heaven and earth as emblematical of the Trinity."[422] Another, by "Anglo-American," is entitled "Copernicus Refuted; or the True Solar System" (Baltimore, 1846). It begins thus:

"One of these must go, the other stand still,
It matters not which, so choose at your will;
But when you find one already stuck fast,
You've only got Hobson's choice left at last."

This writer admits the earth's axial rotation, but declares the earth is fixed as a pivot in the center of the universe, because the poles of the earth are fixed and immovable, and that the sun as in the Tychonic scheme encircles the earth and is itself encircled by five planets.[423] His account of the origin of the Copernican system is noteworthy: it was originated by Pythagoras and his deciples but lay neglected because it was held to be untenable in their time; it was "revived when learning was at its lowest ebb by a monk in his cloister, Copernicus, who in ransacking the contents of the monastery happened to lay his hands on the MS. and then published it to the world with all its blunders and imperfections!"[424] One might remark that the Anglo-American's own learning was at very low ebb.

The Tychonic scheme was revived also some years later by a Dane, Zytphen (1856).[425] Three years after, an assembly of Lutheran clergy met together at Berlin to protest against "science falsely so-called,"[426] but were brought into ridicule by Pastor Knap's denunciations of the Copernican theory as absolutely incompatible with belief in the Bible. A Carl Schoepffer had taken up the defense of the Tychonic scheme in Berlin before this (1854) and by 1868 his lecture was in its seventh edition. In it he sought to prove that the earth revolves neither upon its own axis nor yet about the sun. He had seen Foucault's pendulum demonstration of the earth's movement, but he held that something else, as yet unexplained, caused the deviation of the pendulum, and that the velocity of the heavens would be no more amazing than the almost incredible velocity of light or of electricity.[427] His lecture, curiously enough, fell into the hands of the late General John Watts de Peyster of New York, who had it translated and published in 1900 together with a supplement by Frank Allaben.[428] Both these gentlemen accepted its scientific views and deductions, but the General refused to go as far as his colleague in the latter's enthusiastic acceptance of the verbal inspiration of the Scriptures as a result of these statements.[429] A few months later, they published a supplementary pamphlet claiming to prove the possibility of the sun's velocity by the analogy of the velocity of certain comets.[430] A Professor J.R. Lange of California (a German), attracted by these documents, sent them his own lucubrations on this subject. He considered Newton's doctrine of universal attraction "nonsense," and had "absolute proof" in the fixity of the Pole Star that the earth does not move.[431] In a letter to General de Peyster, he wrote: "Let us hope and pray that the days of the pernicious Copernican system may be numbered,"[432] — but he did not specify why he considered it pernicious. The General was nearly eighty years old when he became interested in these matters, and he did not live long thereafter to defend his position. His biographers make no mention of it. The other men seem almost obsessed, especially Lange; — like the Italian painter, Sindico, who bombarded the director of the Paris Observatory in 1878 with many letters protesting against the Copernican system.[433]

German writers, whether Lutherans or not, appear to have opposed the system more often in the last century than have the writers of other nationalities. Besides those already mentioned, one proposed an ingenious scheme in which the sun moves through space followed by the planets as a comet is by its tail, the planets revolving in a plane perpendicular to that of the sun's path. A diagram of it would be cone-shaped. He included in this pamphlet, besides a list of his own books, (all published in Leipsic), a list of twenty-six titles from 1758 to 1883, books and pamphlets evidently opposed in whole or in part to the modern astronomy, and seventeen of these were in German or printed in Germany.[434] In this country at St. Louis was issued an *Astronomische Unterredung* (1873) by J.C.W.L.; according to the late President White, a bitter attack on modern astronomy and a decision by the Scriptures that the earth is the principal body of the universe, that it stands fixed, and that the sun and the moon only serve to light it.[435]

Such statements are futile in themselves nowadays, and are valuable only to illustrate the advance of modern thought of which these are the little eddies. While modern astronomers know far more than Copernicus even dreamed of, much of his work still holds true today. The world was slow to accept his system because of tradition, authority, so-called common sense, and its supposed incompatibility with scriptural passages. Catholic and Protestant alike opposed it on these grounds; but because of its organization and authority, the Roman Catholic Church had far greater power and could more successfully hinder and delay its acceptance than could the Protestants. Consequently the system won favor slowly at first through the indifference of the authorities, then later in spite of their active antagonism. Scholars believed it long before the universities were permitted to teach it; and the rationalist movement of the 18th century, the revolt against a superstitious religion, helped to overturn the age-old conception of the heavens and to bring Newtonian-Copernicanism into general acceptance.

The elements of this traditional conception are summarized in the fifth book of Bodin's *Universæ Naturæ Theatrum*, a scholar's account of astronomy at the close of the sixteenth century.[436] Man in his terrestrial habitation occupies the center of a universe created solely to serve him, God presides over all from the Empyrean above, sending forth his messengers the angels to guide and control the heavenly bodies. Such had been the thought of Christians for more than a thousand years. Then came the influence of a new science. Tycho Brahe "broke the crystal spheres of Aristotle"[437] by his study of the comet of 1572; Galileo's telescopes revealed many stars hitherto unknown, and partly solved the mysteries of the Milky Way; Kepler's laws explained the courses of the planets, and Newton's discovery of the universal application of the forces of attraction relieved the angels of their duties among the heavens. Thinkers like Bruno proposed the possibility of other systems and universes besides the solar one in which the earth belongs. And thus not only did man shrink in importance in his own eyes; but his conception of the heavens changed from that of a finite place inexplicably controlled by the mystical beings of a supernatural world, to one of vast and infinite spaces traversed by bodies whose density and mass a man could calculate, whose movements he could foretell, and whose very substance he could analyze by the science of today. This dissolution of superstition, especially in regard to comets was notably rapid and complete after the comet of 1680.[438] Thus the rationalist movement with the new science opened men's minds to a universe composed of familiar substances and controlled by known or knowable laws with no tinge remaining of the supernatural. Today a man's theological beliefs are not shaken by the discovery of a new satellite or even a new planet, and the appearance of a new comet merely provides the newspaper editor with the subject of a passing jest.

Yet it was fully one hundred and fifty years after the publication of the *De Revolutionibus* before its system met with the general approval of scholars as well as of mathematicians; then nearly a generation more had to elapse before it was openly taught even at Oxford where the Roman Catholic and Lutheran Churches had no control. During the latter part of this period, readers were often left free to decide for themselves as to the relative merits of the Tychonic and Copernican or Copernican-Cartesian schemes. But it took fully fifty years and more, besides, before these ideas had won general acceptance by the common people, so wedded were they to the traditional view through custom and a superstitious reverence for the Bible. Briefly then, the *De Revolutionibus* appeared in 1543; and quietly won some supporters, notably Bruno, Kepler and Galileo; the Congregations of the Index specifically opposed it in 1616 and 1633; however it continued to spread among scholars and others with the aid of Cartesianism for another fifty years till the appearance of Newton's *Principia* in 1687. Then its acceptance rapidly became general even in Catholic Europe, till it was almost a commonplace in England by

1743, two hundred years after its first formal promulgation, and had become strong enough in Europe to cause the Congregations in 1757 to modify their stand. Thereafter opposition became a curiosity rather than a significant fact. Only the Roman Church officially delayed its recognition of the new astronomy till the absurdity of its obsolete position was brought home to it by Canon Settele's appeal in 1820. Fifteen years later the last trace of official condemnation was removed, a little over two hundred years after the decrees had first been issued, and just before Bessel's discovery of stellar parallax at length answered one of the strongest and oldest arguments against the system. Since then have come many *apologias* in explanation and extenuation of the Church's decided stand in this matter for so many generations.

Though Galileo himself was forced to his knees, unable to withstand his antagonists, his work lived on after him; he and Copernicus, together with Kepler and Newton stand out both as scientists and as leaders in the advance of intellectual enlightenment. The account of their work and that of their less well-known supporters, compared with that of their antagonists, proves the truth of the ancient Greek saying which Rheticus used as the motto for the *Narratio Prima*, the first widely known account of the Copernican system: "One who intends to philosophize must be free in mind."

# APPENDIX A.

## PTOLEMY: *Syntaxis Mathematica (Almagest)*

"That the earth has no movement of rotation," in *Opera Quæ Exstant Omnia*, edidit Heiberg, Leipsic, 1898, Bk. I, sec. 7: (I, 21-25); compared with the translation into French by Halma, Paris, 1813.

By proofs similar to the preceding, it is shown that the earth cannot be transported obliquely nor can it be moved away from the center. For, if that were so, all those things would take place which would happen if it occupied any other point than that of the center. It seems unnecessary to me, therefore, to seek out the cause of attraction towards the center when it is once evident from the phenomena themselves, that the earth occupies the center of the universe and that all heavy bodies are borne towards it; and this will be readily understood if it is remembered that the earth has been demonstrated to have a spherical shape, and according to what we have said, is placed at the center of the universe, for the direction of the fall of heavy bodies (I speak of their own motions) is always and everywhere perpendicular to an uncurved plane drawn tangent to the point of intersection. Obviously these bodies would all meet at the center if they were not stopped by the surface, since a straight line drawn to the center is perpendicular to a plane tangent to the sphere at that point.

Those who consider it a paradox that a mass like the earth is supported on nothing, yet not moved at all, appear to me to argue according to the preconceptions they get from what they see happening to small bodies about them, and not according to what is characteristic of the universe as a whole, and this is the cause of their mistake. For I think that such a thing would not have seemed wonderful to them any longer if they had perceived that the earth, great as it is, is merely a point in comparison to the surrounding body of the heaven. They would find that it is possible for the earth, being infinitely small relative to the universe, to be held in check and fixed by the forces exercised over it equally and following similar directions by the universe, which is infinitely great and composed of similar parts. There is neither up nor down in the universe, for that cannot be imagined in a sphere. As to the bodies which it encloses, by a consequence of their nature it happens that those that are light and subtle are as though blown by the wind to the outside and to the circumference, and seem to appear to us to go *up*, because that is how we speak of the space above our heads that envelops us. It happens on the other hand that heavy bodies and those composed of dense parts are drawn towards the middle as towards a center, and appear to us to fall *down*, because that it is the word we apply to what is beneath our feet in the direction of the center of the earth. But one should believe that they are checked around this center by the retarding effect of shock and of friction. It would be admitted then that the entire mass of the earth, which is considerable in comparison to the bodies falling on it, could receive these in their fall without acquiring the slightest motion from the shock of their weight or of their velocity. But if the earth had a movement which was common to it and to all other heavy bodies, it would soon seemingly outstrip them as a result of its weight, thus leaving the animals and the other heavy bodies without other support than the air, and would soon touch the limits of the heaven itself. All these consequences would seem most ridiculous if one were only even imagining them.

There are those who, while they admit these arguments because there is nothing to oppose them, pretend that nothing prevents the supposition, for instance, that if the sky is motionless, the earth might turn on its axis from west to east, making this revolution once a day or in a very little less time, or that, if they both turn, it is around the same axis, as we have said, and in a manner conformable to the relations between them which we have observed.

It has escaped these people that in regard to the appearances of the planets themselves, nothing perhaps prevents the earth from having the simpler motion; but they do not realize how very ridiculous their opinion is in view of what takes place around us and in the air. For if we grant them that the lightest things and those composed of the subtlest parts do not move, which would be contrary to nature, while those that are in the air move visibly more swiftly than those that are terrestrial; if we grant them that the most solid and heavy bodies have a swift, steady movement of their own, though it is true however that they obey impelling forces only with difficulty; they would be obliged to admit that the earth by its revolution has a movement more rapid than the movements taking place around it, since it would make so great a circuit in so short a time. Thus the bodies which do not rest on it would appear always to have a motion contrary to its own, and neither the clouds, nor any missile or flying bird would appear to go towards the east, for the earth would always outstrip them in this direction, and would anticipate them by its own movement towards the east, with the result that all the rest would appear to move backwards towards the west.

If they should say that the atmosphere is carried along by the earth with the same speed as the earth's own revolution, it would be no less true that the bodies contained therein would not have the same velocity. Or if they were swept along with the air, no longer would anything seem to precede or to follow, but all would always appear stationary, and neither in flight nor in throwing would any ever advance or retreat. That is, however, what we see happening, since neither the retardation nor the acceleration of anything is traceable to the movement of the earth.

# APPENDIX B.

## "TO HIS HOLINESS, PAUL III, SUPREME PONTIFF, PREFACE BY NICHOLAS COPERNICUS TO HIS BOOKS ON REVOLUTIONS."

(A translation of the *Præfatio* in Copernicus: *De Revolutionibus*; -8.)

"I can certainly well believe, most holy Father, that, while mayhap a few will accept this my book which I have written concerning the revolutions of the spheres of the world, ascribing certain motions to the sphere of the earth, people will clamor that I ought to be cast out at once for such an opinion. Nor are my ideas so pleasing to me that I will not carefully weigh what others decide concerning them. And although I know that the meditations of philosophers are remote from the opinions of the unlearned, because it is their aim to seek truth in all things so far as it is permitted by God to the human reason, nevertheless I think that opinions wholly alien to the right ought to be driven out. Thus when I considered with myself what an absurd fairy-tale people brought up in the opinion, sanctioned by many ages, that the earth is motionless in the midst of the heaven, as if it were the center of it, would think it if I were to assert on the contrary that the earth is moved; I hesitated long whether I would give to the light my commentaries composed in proof of this motion, or whether it would indeed be more satisfactory to follow the example of the Pythagoreans and various others who were wont to pass down the mysteries of philosophy not by books, but from hand to hand only to their friends and relatives, as the letter of Lysis to Hipparchus proves. [439] But verily they seemed to me not to have done this, as some think, from any dislike to spreading their teachings, but lest the most beautiful things and those investigated with much earnestness by great men, should be despised by those to whom spending good work on any book is a trouble unless they make profit by it; or if they are incited to the liberal study of philosophy by the exhortations and the example of others, yet because of the stupidity of their wits they are no more busily engaged among philosophers than drones among bees. When therefore I had pondered these matters, the scorn which was to be feared on account of the novelty and the absurdity of the opinion impelled me for that reason to set aside entirely the book already drawn up.

"But friends, in truth, have brought me forth into the light again, though I long hesitated and am still reluctant; among these the foremost was Nicholas Schönberg, Cardinal of Capua, celebrated in all fields of scholarship. Next to him is that scholar, my very good friend, Tiedeman Giese, Bishop of Culm, most learned in all sacred matters, (as he is), and in all good sciences. He has repeatedly urged me and, sometimes even with censure, implored me to publish this book and to suffer it to see the light at last, as it has lain hidden by me not for nine years alone, but also into the fourth 'novenium'. Not a few other scholars of eminence also pleaded with me, exhorting me that I should no longer refuse to contribute my book to the common service of mathematicians on account of an imagined dread. They said that however absurd in many ways this my doctrine of the earth's motion might now appear, so much the greater would be the admiration and goodwill after people had seen by the publications of my commentaries the mists of absurdities rolled away by the most lucid demonstrations. Brought to this hope, therefore, by these pleaders, I at last permitted my friends, as they had long besought me, to publish this work.

"But perhaps your Holiness will not be so shocked that I have dared to bring forth into the light these my lucubrations, having spent so much work in elaborating them, that I did not hesitate even to commit to a book my conclusions about the earth's motion, but that you will particularly wish to hear from me how it came into my mind to dare to imagine any motion of the earth, contrary to the accepted opinion of mathematicians and in like manner contrary to common sense. So I do not wish to conceal from your Holiness that nothing else moved me to consider some other explanation for the motions of the spheres of the universe than what I knew, namely that mathematicians did not agree among themselves in their examinations of these things. For in the first place, they are so completely undecided concerning the motion of the sun and of the moon that they could not observe and prove the constant length of the great year.[440] Next, in determining the motions of both these and the five other planets, they did not use the same principles and assumptions or even the same demonstrations of the appearances of revolutions and motions. For some used only homocentric circles; others, eccentrics and epicycles, which on being questioned about, they themselves did not fully comprehend. For those who put their trust in homocentrics, although they proved that other diverse motions could be derived from these, nevertheless they could by no means decide on any thing certain which in the least corresponded to the phenomena. But these who devised eccentrics, even though they seem for the most part to have represented apparent motions by a number [of eccentrics] suitable to them, yet in the meantime they have admitted quite a few which appear to contravene the first principles of equality of motion. Another notable thing, that there is a definite symmetry between the form of the universe and its parts, they could not devise or construct from these; but it is with them as if a man should take from different places, hands, feet, a head and other members, in the best way possible indeed, but in no way comparable to a single body, and in no respect corresponding to each other, so that a monster rather than a man would be constructed from them. Thus in the process of proof, which they call a system, they are found to have passed over some essential, or to have admitted some thing both strange and scarcely relevant. This would have been least likely to have happened to them if they had followed definite principles. For if the hypotheses they assumed were not fallacious, everything which followed out of them would have been verified beyond a doubt. However obscure may be what I now say, nevertheless in its own place it will be made more clear.

"When therefore I had long considered this uncertainty of traditional mathematics, it began to weary me that no more definite explanation of the movement of the world machine established in our behalf by the best and most systematic builder of all, existed among the philosophers who had studied so exactly in other respects the minutest details in regard to the sphere. Wherefore I took upon myself the task of re-reading the books of all the philosophers which I could obtain, to seek out whether any one had ever conjectured that the motions of the spheres of the universe were other than they supposed who taught mathematics in the schools. And I found first that, according to Cicero, Nicetas had thought the earth was moved. Then later I discovered according to Plutarch that certain others had held the same opinion; and in order that this passage may be available to all, I wish to write it down here:

> "But while some say the earth stands still, Philolaus the Pythagorean held that it is moved about the element of fire in an oblique circle, after the same manner of motion that the sun and moon have. Heraclides of Pontus and Ecphantus the Pythagorean assign a motion to the earth, not progressive, but after the manner of a wheel being carried on its own axis. Thus the earth, they say, turns itself upon its own center from west to east."[441]

When from this, therefore, I had conceived its possibility I myself also began to meditate upon the mobility of the earth. And although the opinion seemed absurd, yet because I knew the liberty had been accorded to others before me of imagining whatsoever circles they pleased to explain the phenomena of the stars, I thought I also might readily be allowed to experiment whether, by supposing the earth to have some motion, stronger demonstrations than those of the others could be found as to the revolution of the celestial sphere.

Thus, supposing these motions which I attribute to the earth later on in this book, I found at length by much and long observation, that if the motions of the other planets were added to the rotation of the earth and calculated as for the revolution of that planet, not only the phenomena of the others followed from this, but also it so bound together both the order and magnitude of all the planets and the spheres and the heaven itself, that in no single part could one thing be altered without confusion among the other parts and in all the universe. Hence, for this reason, in the course of this work I have followed this system, so that in the first book I describe all the positions of the spheres together with the motions I attribute to the earth; thus this book contains a kind of general disposition of the universe. Then in the remaining books, I bring together the motions of the other planets and all the spheres with the mobility of the earth, so that it can thence be inferred to what extent the motions and appearances of the other planets and spheres can be solved by attributing motion to the earth. Nor do I doubt that skilled and scholarly mathematicians will agree with me if, what philosophy requires from the beginning, they will examine and judge, not casually but deeply, what I have gathered together in this book to prove these things. In order that learned and unlearned may alike see that in no way whatsoever I evade judgment, I prefer to dedicate these my lucubrations to your Holiness rather than to any one else; especially because even in this very remote corner of the earth in which I live, you are held so very eminent by reason of the dignity of your position and also for your love of all letters and of mathematics that, by your authority and your decision, you can easily suppress the malicious attacks of calumniators, even though proverbially there is no remedy against the attacks of sycophants.

rent circulos ad demonſtrandum phænomena aſtrorum . Exiſti-
mavi mihi quoque facile permitti, ut experirem, an poſito terræ ali-
quo motu firmiores demonſtrationes, quam illorum eſſent, inveni-
ri in revolutione orbium cæleſtium poſſent.

Atque ita ego poſitis motibus, quos terræ infra in opere tribuo,
multa & longa obſervatione tandem reperi, quod ſi reliquorum ſyderum errantium motus, ad terræ circulationem conferantur, &
ſupputentur pro cujuſque ſyderis revolutione, non modo illorum
phænomena inde ſequantur, ſed & ſyderum atque orbium omnium
ordines, magnitudines, & cælum ipſum ita connectat , ut in nulla
ſui parte poſſit transponi aliquid, ſine reliquarum partium, ac totius
univerſitatis confuſione. Proinde quoque & in progreſſu operis
hunc ſecutus ſum ordinem ut in primo libro deſcribam omnes poſi-
tiones orbium, cum terræ, quos ei tribuo, motibus, ut is liber con-
tineat communem quaſi conſtitutionem univerſi. In reliquis vero
libris poſtea conſero reliquorum ſyderum atque omnium orbium
motus, cum terræ mobilitate, ut inde colligi poſſit, quatenus reliquorum ſyderum atque orbium motus & apparentiæ ſalvari poſſint,
ſi ad terræ motus conferantur. Neque dubito, quin ingenioſi atque
docti Mathematici mihi aſtipulaturi ſint, ſi quod hæc philoſophia in
primis exigit, non obiter, ſed penitus, ea quæ ad harum rerum de-
monſtrationem a me in hoc opere, adferuntur, cognoſcere atque
expendere voluerint. Vt vero pariter docti atque indocti viderent,
me nullius omnino ſubterfugere judicium, malui tuæ Sanctitati,
quam cuiquam alteri has meas lucubrationes dedicare , propterea
quod & in hoc remotiſſ. angulo terræ, in quo ego ago, ordinis digni-
tate, & literarum omnium atque Mathematices etiam amore, emi-
nentiſſ. habearis, ut facile tua authoritate & judicio calumniantium
morſus reprimere poſſis, etſi in proverbio ſit, non eſſe remedium
adverſus Sycophantæ morſum.

Si fortaſſe erunt ματαιολογοι, qui cum omnium Mathematum igna-
ri ſint, tamen de illis judicium ſibi ſumunt, propter aliquem loſum
_ _ _ male ad ſuum propoſitum detortum, auſi fuerint meum
hoc inſtitutum reprehendere ac inſectari: illos nihil moror, adeo ut
etiam illorum judicium tanquam _ _ _ contemnam. Non
enim obſcurum eſt Lactantium, celebrem alioqui ſcriptorem, ſed
Mathematicum parum, adm odum pueriliter de forma terræ loqui,
cum deridet eos, qui terram globi formam habere prodiderunt.

(∴) 3          Ita-

A photographic facsimile (reduced) of a page from Mulier's
edition (1617) as "corrected" according to the *Monitum* of the
Congregations in 1620. The first writer merely underlined the
passage with marginal comment that this was to be deleted by
ecclesiastical order. The second writer scratched out the passage
and referred to the second volume of Riccioli's *Almagestum
Novum* for the text of the order. The earlier writer was probably
the librarian of the Florentine convent from which this book came,
and wrote this soon after 1620. The later writer did his work after

1651, when Riccioli's book was published. This copy of the *De Revolutionibus* is now in the Dartmouth College Library.

If perchance there should be foolish speakers who, together with those ignorant of all mathematics, will take it upon themselves to decide concerning these things, and because of some place in the Scriptures wickedly distorted to their purpose, should dare to assail this my work, they are of no importance to me, to such an extent do I despise their judgment as rash. For it is not unknown that Lactantius, the writer celebrated in other ways but very little in mathematics, spoke somewhat childishly of the shape of the earth when he derided those who declared the earth had the shape of a ball.[442] So it ought not to surprise students if such should laugh at us also. Mathematics is written for mathematicians to whom these our labors, if I am not mistaken, will appear to contribute something even to the ecclesiastical state the headship of which your Holiness now occupies. For it is not so long ago under Leo X when the question arose in the Lateran Council about correcting the Ecclesiastical Calendar. It was left unsettled then for this reason alone, that the length of the year and of the months and the movements of the sun and moon had not been satisfactorily determined. From that time on, I have turned my attention to the more accurate observation of these, at the suggestion of that most celebrated scholar, Father Paul, a bishop from Rome, who was the leader then in that matter. What, however, I may have achieved in this, I leave to the decision of your Holiness especially, and to all other learned mathematicians. And lest I seem to your Holiness to promise more about the value of this work than I can perform, I now pass on to the undertaking.

# APPENDIX C.

The Drama of Universal Nature: in which are considered the efficient causes and the ends of all things, discussed in a connected series of five books, by Jean Bodin, (Frankfort, 1597).

*Book V*: On the Celestial Bodies: their number, movement, size, harmony and distances compared with themselves and with the earth. Sections 1 and 10 (in part) and 12 (entire).

Bodin, Jean: *Universæ Naturæ Theatrum in quo rerum omnium effectrices causa et fines contemplantur, et continuæ series quinque libris discutiuntur.* Frankfort, 1597. Book V translated into English by the writer and compared with the French translation by François de Fougerolles, (Lyons, 1597).

*Section 1*: On the definition and the number of the spheres.

Mystagogue: ... Now to prove that the heavens have a nature endowed with intelligence I need no other argument than that by which Theophrastus and Alexander prove they are living, for, they say, if the heavens did not have intelligence, they would be greatly inferior in dignity and excellence to men. That is why Aben-Ezra,[443] having interpreted the Hebrew of these two words of the Psalm: "The heavens declare," has written that the phrase *Sapperim* (declare) in the judgment of all Hebrews is appropriate to such great intelligence. Also he who said "When the morning stars sang together and shouted for joy,"[444] indicated a power endowed with intelligence, as did the Master of Wisdom[445] also when he said that God created the heavens with intelligence.

Theodore. I have learned in the schools that the spheres are not moved of themselves but that they have separate intelligences who incite them to movement.

Myst. That is the doctrine of Aristotle. But Theophrastus and Alexander,[446] (when they teach that the spheres are animated bodies) explain adequately that the spheres are agitated by their own coëssential soul. For if the sky were turned by an intelligence external to it, its movement would be accidental with the result that it, and the stars with it, would not be moved otherwise, than as a body without soul. But accidental motion is violent. And nothing violent in nature can be of long duration. On the contrary there is nothing of longer duration, nor more constant, than the movement of the heavens.

Theo. What do you call fixed stars?

Myst. Celestial beings who are gifted with intelligence and with light, and who are in continual motion. This is sufficiently indicated by the words of Daniel[447] when he wrote, that the souls of those who have walked justly in this life, and who have brought men back to the path of virtue, all have their seat and dwelling (like the gleaming stars) among the heavens. By these words one can plainly understand the essence and figure of the angels as well as of the celestial beings; for while other beings have their places in this universe assigned to them for their habitation, as the fish the sea, the cattle the fields, and the wild beasts the mountains and forests, even as Origen,[448] Eusebius, and Diodorus say, so the stars are assigned positions in the heavens. This can also be understood by the curtains of the tabernacle which Moses, the great Lawgiver, had ornamented with the images of cherubim showing that the heavens were indicated by the angelic faces of the stars. While St. Augustine,[449] Jerome,[450] Thomas Aquinas[451] and Scotus most fitly called this universe a being, nevertheless Albertus, Damascenus, and Thomas Aquinas deny that the heavenly bodies are animated. But Thomas Aquinas shows himself in this inconsistent and contradictory, for he confesses that spiritual substances are united with the heavenly bodies, which could not be unless they were united in the same hypostasis of an animated body. If this body is animated, it must necessarily be living and either rational or irrational. If, on the other hand, this spiritual substance does not make the same hypostasis with the celestial body, it will necessarily be that the movement of the sky is accidental, as coming from the mover outside to the thing moved, no more nor less than the movement of a wheel comes from the one who turns it: As this is absurd, what follows from it is necessarily absurd also.

Theo. How many spheres are there?

Myst. It is difficult to determine their number because of the variety of opinions among the authorities, each differing from the other, and because of the inadequacy of the proofs of such things. For Eudoxus has stated that the spheres with their deferents are not more than three and twenty in number. Calippus has put it at thirty, and Aristotle[452] at forty-seven, which Alexander Aphrodisiensis[453] has amended by adding to it two more on the advice of Sosigenes. Ptolemy holds that there are 31 celestial spheres not including the bodies of the planets. Johan Regiomontanus says 33, an opinion which is followed by nearly all, because in the time of Ptolemy they did not yet know that the eighth sphere and all the succeeding ones are carried around by the movement of the trepidation. Thus he held that the moon has five orbits, Mercury six, Venus, Mars, Jupiter, and Saturn each four, aside from the bodies of the planets themselves, for beyond these are still the spheres and deferents of the eighth and ninth spheres. But Copernicus, reviving Eudoxus' idea, held that the earth moved around the motionless sun; and he has also removed the epicycles with the result that he has greatly reduced their number, so that one can scarcely find eight spheres remaining.

Theo. What should one do with such a variety of opinions?

Myst. Have recourse to the sacred fountain of the Hebrews to search out the mysteries of a thing so deeply hidden from man; for from them we may obtain an absolutely certain decision. The Tabernacle which the great Lawgiver Moses ordered to be made[454] was like the Archetype of the universe, with its ten curtains placed around it each decorated with the figures of cherubim thus representing the ten heavens with the beauty of their resplendent stars. And even though Aben-Ezra did not know of the movement of trepidation, nevertheless he interpreted this passage, "The heavens are the work of Thy fingers" as indicating the number of the ten celestial spheres. The Pythagoreans seem also to have agreed upon the same number since, besides the earth and the eight heavens, they imagine a sphere Antichthon because they did not then clearly understand the celestial movements. They thought however, all should be embraced in the tenth.

Theo. The authority of such writers has indeed so great weight with me that I place their statements far in advance of the arguments of all others. Nevertheless if it can be done, I should wish to have this illustrated and confirmed by argument in order to satisfy those who believe nothing except on absolute proof.

Myst. It can indeed be proved that there are ten mobile spheres in which the fiery bodies accomplish their regular courses. Yet by these arguments that ultimate, motionless sphere which embraces and encircles all from our terrestrial abode to its circumference within its crystalline self, encompassing plainly the utmost shores and limits of the universe, cannot be proved. For as it has been shown before [in Book I] the elemental world was inundated by celestial waters from above. Nor can it apparently be included in the number of the spheres since (as we will point out later) as great a distance exists between it and the nearest sphere as between the ocean and the starry heaven. Furthermore it has been said before that the essence of the spheres consists of fire and water which is not fitting for the celestial waters above.

Theo. By what arguments then can it be proved there are ten spheres?

Myst. The ancients knew well that there were the seven spheres of the planets, and an eighth sphere of the fixed stars which, down to the time of Eudoxus and Meto, they thought had but one simple movement. These men were the first who perceived by observation that the fixed stars were carried backward quite contrary to the movement of the Primum Mobile. After them came Timochares, Hipparchus, and Menelaus, and later Ptolemy, who confirmed these observations perceiving that the fixed stars (which people had hitherto thought were fixed in their places) had been separated from their station. For this reason they thought best to add a ninth sphere to the eight inferior ones. Much later an Arabian and a Spanish king, Mensor and Alphonse, great students of the celestial sciences, in their observations noticed that the eighth sphere with the seven following moved in turning from the north to the east, then towards the south, and so to the west, finally returning to the north, and that such a movement was completed in 7000 years. This Johannus Regiomontanus, a Franconian, has proved, with a skill hitherto equalled only by that of those who proved the ninth sphere, which travels from west to east. From this it is necessarily concluded that there are ten spheres.

Theo. Why so?

Myst. Because every natural body[455] has but one movement which is its own by nature; all others are either voluntary or through violence, contrary to the nature of a mobile object; for just as a stone cannot of its own impulse ascend and descend, so one and the same sphere cannot of itself turn from the east to the west and from the west to the east and still less from the north to the south and south to north.

Theo. What then?

Myst. It follows from this that the extremely rapid movement by which all the spheres are revolved in twenty-four hours, belongs to the Primum Mobile, which we call the tenth sphere, and which carries with it all the nine lesser spheres; that the second or planetary movement, that is, from west to east, is communicated to the lesser spheres and belongs to the ninth sphere; that the third movement, resembling a person staggering, belongs to the eighth sphere with which it affects the other lesser spheres and makes them stagger in a measure outside of the poles, axes and centres of the greater spheres.

Section 10: On the position of the universe according to its divisions.

\* \* \* \*

Theo. Does it not also concern Physics to discuss those things that lie outside the universe?

Myst. If there were any natural body beyond the heavens, most assuredly it would concern Physics, that is, the observer and student of nature. But in the book of Origins,[456] the Master workman is said to have separated the waters and placed the firmament in between them. The Hebrew philosophers declare that the crystalline sphere which Ezekiel[457] called the great crystal and upon which he saw God seated, as he wrote, is as far beyond the farthermost heaven as our ocean is far from that heaven, and that this orb is motionless and therefore is called God's throne. For "seat" implies quiet and tranquility which could be proper for none other than the one immobile and immutable God. This is far more probable and likely than Aristotle's absurd idea, unworthy the name of a philosopher, by which he placed the eternal God in a moving heaven as if He were its source of motion and in such fashion that He was constrained of necessity to move it. We have already refuted this idea. It has also been shown that these celestial waters full of fertility and productiveness sometimes are spread abroad more widely and sometimes less so, as though obviously restrained, whence the heavens are said to be closed[458] and roofed[459] with clouds or that floods burst forth out of the heaven to inundate the earth. Finally we read in the Holy Scriptures that the eternal God is seated upon the flood.

Theo. Why then are not eleven spheres counted?

Myst. Because the crystalline sphere is said to have been separated from the inferior waters by the firmament, and it therefore cannot be called a heaven. Furthermore motion is proper to all the heavens, but the crystalline one is stationary. That is why Rabi Akiba called[460] it a marble counterpart of the universe. This also is signified in the construction of the altar which was covered with a pavilion in addition to its ten curtains for, as it is stated elsewhere,[461] God covers the heavens with clouds, and the Scriptures often make mention of the waters beyond the heavens.[462] There are those, however, who teach that the Hebrew word *Scamajim* may be applied only to a dual number, so that they take it to mean the crystalline sphere and the starry one. But I think those words in Solomon's speech[463] "the heaven of heaven, and the heavens of the heavens" refer in the singular to the crystalline sphere, in the plural to the ten lesser spheres.

Theo. It does not seem so marvelous to me that an aqueous or crystalline sphere exists beyond the ten spheres, as that it is as far beyond the furthermost sphere as the ocean is far this side of it, that is, as astrologists teach, 1040 terrestrial diameters.

Myst. It is written most plainly that the firmament holds the middle place between the two waters. Therefore God is called[464] in Hebrew *Helion*, the Sun, that is, the Most High, and under His feet the heaven is spread like a crystal,[465] although He is neither excluded nor included in any part of the universe, it is however consistent with His Majesty to be above all the spheres and to fill heaven and earth with His infinite power as Isaiah[466] indicated when he writes: "His train filled the temple;" it is the purest and simplest act, the others are brought about by forces and powers. He alone is incorporeal, others are corporeal or joined to bodies. He alone is eternal, others according to their nature are transitory and fleeting unless they are strengthened by the Creator's might; wherefore the Chaldean interpreter is seen everywhere to have used the words, Majesty, Glory or Power in place of the presence of God.

Theo. Nevertheless so vast and limitless a space must be filled with air or fire, since there are no spheres there, nor will nature suffer any vacuum.

Myst. If then the firmament occupies the middle position between the two waters, then by this hypothesis you must admit that the space beyond the spheres is empty of elemental and celestial bodies; otherwise you would have to admit that the last sphere extends on even to the crystalline orb, which can in no way be reconciled with the Holy Scriptures and still less with reason because of the incredible velocity of this sphere. Therefore it is far more probable that this space is filled with angels.

Theo. Is there some medium between God and the angels which shares in the nature of both?

Myst. What is incorporeal and indivisible cannot communicate any part of its essence to another; for if a creature had any part of the divine essence, it would be all God, since God neither has parts nor can be divided, therefore He must be separated from all corporeal contact or intermixture.

*Section 12*: On guardian angels.

Theo. What then in corporeal nature is closest to God?

Myst. The two Seraphim, who stand near the eternal Creator,[467] and who are said to have six wings, two wherewith to fly, the others to cover head and feet. By this is signified the admirable swiftness with which they fulfill His commands, yet head and feet are veiled for so the purpose of their origin and its earliest beginning are not known to us. Also they have eyes scattered in all parts of their bodies to indicate that nothing is hidden from them. And they also pour oil for lighting through a funnel into the seven-branched candlestick; that is, strength and power are poured forth by the Creator to the seven planets, so that we should turn from created things to the worship and love of the Creator.

Theo. Since nothing is more fitting for the Divine goodness than to create, to generate, and to pile up good things for all, whence comes the destruction of the world and the ruin of all created things?

Myst. It is true Plato and Aristotle attributed the cause of all ills to the imperfection of matter in which they thought was some *kakopoion*,[468] but that is absurd since it is distinctly written: All that God had made was good, or as the Hebrews express it, beautiful,—so evil is nothing-else than the absence[469] or privation of good.

Theo. Can not wicked angels be defined without privation since they are corporeal essences?

Myst. Anything that exists is said to be good and to be a participant by its existence in the divine goodness; and even as in a well regulated Republic, executioners, lictors, and corpse-bearers are no less necessary than magistrates, judges and overseers; so in the Republic of this world, for the generation, management and guardianship of things God has gathered together angels as leaders and directors for all the celestial places, for the elements, for living beings, for plants, for minerals, for states, provinces, families and individuals. And not only has He done this, but He has also assigned His servants, lictors, avengers and others to places where they may do nothing without His order, nor inflict any punishment upon wicked men unless the affair has been known fully and so decided. Thus God is said[470] to have made Leviathan, which is the outflow of Himself, that is, the natural rise and fall of all things. "I have created a killer,"[471] He said, "to destroy," and so also Behemoth, and the demons cleaving to him, which are often called ravens, eagles and lions, and which are said to beg their food of God, that is, the taking of vengeance upon the wicked whose punishment and death they feed upon as upon ordinary fare. From these, therefore, or rather from ourselves, come death, pestilence, famine, war and those things we call ills, and not from the Author of all good things except by accident. For so God says of Himself:[472] "I am the God making good and creating evil, making light and creating darkness." For when He withdraws His spirit, evil follows the good; when He takes the light away, darkness is created; as when one removes the pillars of a building, the ruin of a house follows. If He takes the vital spark away, death follows; nor can He be said to do evil[473] to anyone in taking back what is His own.

Theo. When the Legislator asked Him to disclose His face to his gaze, why did the Architect of the universe and the Author of all things reply: "My face is to be seen by no mortal man, but only my back?"

Myst. This fine allegory signifies that God cannot be known from superior or antecedent causes but from behind His back, that is, from results, for a little later He adds, "I will cover thine eyes with My hand." Thus the hand signifies those works which He has placed before anyone's eyes, and it indicates that He places man not in an obscure corner but in the center of the universe so that He might better and more easily than in heaven contemplate the universe and all His works through the sight of which, as through spectacles, the Sun, that is, God Himself, may be disclosed. And therefore we undertook this disputation concerning nature and natural things, so that even if they are but slightly explained, nevertheless we may attain from this disquisition an imperfect knowledge of the Creator and may break forth in His praises with all our might, that at length by degrees we may be borne on high and be blessed by the Divine reward; for this is indeed the supreme and final good for a man.

Here endeth the Drama of Nature which Jean Bodin wrote while all France was aflame with civil war.

Finis

# APPENDIX D.

## A TRANSLATION OF A LETTER BY THOMAS FEYENS ON THE QUESTION: IS IT TRUE THAT THE HEAVENS ARE MOVED AND THE EARTH IS AT REST? (FEBRUARY, 1619)

(*Thomæ Fieni Epistolica Quæstio*: An verum sit, cœlum moveri et terram quiescere? Londini, 1655.)

To the eminent and noble scholars, Tobias Matthias and George Gays:

IT is proved that the heavens are moved and the earth is stationary: First; by authority; for besides the fact that this is asserted by Aristotle and Ptolemy whom wellnigh all Philosophers and Mathematicians have followed by unanimous consent, except for Copernicus, Bernardus Patricius[474] and a very few others, the Holy Scriptures plainly attest it in at least two places which I have seen. In Joshua,[475] are the words: Steteruntque sol et luna donec ulcisceretur gens de inimicis suis. And a little further on: Stetit itaque sol in medio cœli, et non festinavit occumbere spatio unius diei, et non fuit antea et postea tam longa dies. The Scriptures obviously refer by these words to the motion of the *primum mobile* by which the sun and the moon are borne along in their diurnal course and the day is defined; and it indicates that the heavens are moved as well as the *primum mobile*. Then Ecclesiastes, chapter 1,[476] reads: Generatio præterit, et generatio advenit, terra autem semper stat, oritur sol et occidit, et ad locum suum revertitur.

Secondly, it is proved by reason. All the heavens and stars were made in man's behalf and, with other terrestrial bodies, are the servants of man to warm, light, and vivify him.

This they could not do unless in moving they applied themselves by turns to different parts of the world. And it is more likely that they would apply themselves by their own movement to man and the place in which man lives, than that man should come to them by the movement of his own seat or habitation. For they are the servants of man; man is not their servant; therefore it is more probable that the heavens are moved and the earth is at rest than that the reverse is true.

Thirdly; no probable argument can be thought out from philosophy to prove that the earth is moved and the heavens are at rest. Nor can it be done by mathematics. By saying that the heavens are moved and the earth is at rest, all phenomena of the heavenly bodies can be solved. Just as in the same way in optics all can be solved by saying either that sight comes from the thing to the eye, or that rays go from the eye to the thing seen; so is it in astronomy. Therefore one ought rather to abide in the ancient and general opinion than in one received recently without justification.

Fourthly; the earth is the center of the universe; all the heavenly bodies are observed to be moved around it; therefore it itself ought to be motionless, for anything that moves, it seems, should move around or above something that is motionless.

Fifthly; if the earth is moved in a circle, either it moves that way naturally or by force, either by its own nature or by the nature of another. It is not by its own nature, for straight motion from above downward is natural to it; therefore circular motion could not be natural to it. Further, the earth is a simple body; and a simple body can not have two natural motions of distinct kinds or classes. Nor is it moved by another body; for by what is it moved? One has to say it is moved either by the sun or by some other celestial body; and this cannot be said, since either the sun or that body is said to be at rest or in motion. If it is said to be at rest, then it cannot impart movement to another. If it is said to be in motion, then it can not move the earth, because it ought to move either by a motion similar to its own or the opposite of it. It is not similar, since thus it would be observed to move neutrally as when two boats moving in the same direction, appear not to move but to be at rest. It is not the opposite motion, since nothing could give motion contrary to its own. And because Galileo seems to say, in so far as I have learned from your lordships, that the earth was moved by the sun; I prove anyway that this is not true since the movement of the sun and of the earth ought to be from contrary and distinct poles. The sun, however, can not be the cause of the other's movement because it is moved above different poles. Lastly, the earth follows the motion of no other celestial body; since if it is moved, it moves in 24 hours, and all the other celestial bodies require the space of many days, months and years. Ergo. Finally, if the earth is moved by another, its motion would be violent; but this is absurd, for no violence can be regular and perpetual.

Sixthly; even so it is declared that the earth is moved. Nevertheless, it must be admitted to this that either the planets themselves or their spheres are moved, for in no other way can the diversities of aspects among themselves be solved; nor can a reason be given why the sun does not leave the Ecliptic and the moon does; and how a planet can be stationary or retrograde, high or low, — and many other phenomena. For this reason those who said the earth moved, as Bernardus Patricius and the others said, claimed that the *primum mobile*, forsooth, was stationary and that the earth was moved in its place; yet they could not in the least deny that the planets themselves were moved, but admitted it. That is the reason why both ancient and modern mathematicians, aside from the motion of the *primum mobile*, were forced to admit and consider the peculiar movements of the planets themselves. If therefore it must be acknowledged, and it is certain, that the stars and the celestial bodies are moved; then it is more probable that all movement perceived in the universe belongs rather to the heavenly bodies than to the earth. For if movement were ascribed to all the rest, why for that same reason is not diurnal rotation ascribed rather to the *primum mobile* than to the earth, particularly when our senses seem to decide thus? Although one may well be mistaken, sometimes, concerning other similar movements; yet it is not probable that all ages could be at fault, or should be, about the movements of its most important objects, of course the celestial luminaries.

Seventhly; it is proved by experience. For if the earth is moved, then an arrow shot straight up on high could never fall back to the place whence it was shot, but should fall somewhere many miles away. But this is not so. Ergo.

This can be answered and is so customarily in this way: this does not follow because the air is swept along with the earth, and so, since the air which carries the arrow is turning in the same way with the earth, the arrow also is borne along equally with it, and thus returns to the same spot. This in truth is a pure evasion and a worthless answer for many reasons.

It is falsely observed that the air is moved and by the same motion as the earth. For what should move the earth? Truly, if the air is moved by the same motion as the earth, either it ought to be moved by the earth itself, or by that other which moves the earth, or by itself. It is not moved by itself; since it has another motion, the straight one of course natural to itself, and also since it has a nature, an essence and qualities all different from the nature and the essence of the earth; therefore it could not by its own nature have the same motion as that other, but of necessity ought to have a different one.

Nor is it moved by any other that may move the earth; as that which moves the earth could not at the same time and with like motion move the air. For since the air is different from the earth in essence, in both active and passive qualities, and in kind of substance, it can not receive the impelling force of the acting body, or that force applied in the same way as the earth, and so could not be moved in the same way. The virtues [of bodies] acting and of moving diversely are received by the recipients according to the diversity of their dispositions. Also it can not be moved by the earth; since if it were moved by the earth, it must be said to be moved by force, but such motion appears to be impossible. Ergo. The minor premise is proved: for if air is thus moved by the earth by force the air ought to be moved more rapidly than the earth, because air is larger [than the earth].

For what is outside is larger than what is inside. When, however, what is larger and what is outside is driven around equally rapidly with what is less, and what is inside, then the former is moved much more rapidly. Thus it is true that the sphere of Saturn in its daily course is moved far faster than the sphere of the moon. But it is impossible that the one driven should move more rapidly than the one driving; therefore the air is not moved by the earth's violence. Thus would it be if the air were moved with the earth, or by itself, or by force. Thus far, then, the force of the original argument remains; since of its own motion, indeed, it could not be in every way conformable to the motion of the earth as I have shown; and this because the air differs from the earth in consistency of substance, in qualities and in essence. But the air ought at all events to move more sluggishly than the earth. It follows from this that an arrow shot straight up could not return to its starting point; for the earth, moving like the air, on account of the other's slower rate leaves it behind, and the arrow also which is carried away from it.

Besides, if the air does not move so rapidly as the earth, a man living in a very high tower, however quiet the air, ought then always to feel the strongest wind and the greatest disturbance of the air.

Since mountains and towers are moved with the earth, and the air would not be accompanying them at an equal speed, it would necessarily follow that they would precede the air by cleaving and cutting and ploughing through it which ought to make a great wind perceptible.

Eighthly; if a person stood in some very high tower or other high place and aimed from that tower at some spot of earth perpendicularly below his eye, and allowed a very heavy stone to fall following that perpendicular line, it is absolutely certain that that stone would land upon the spot aimed at perpendicularly underneath. But if the earth is moved, it would be impossible for the stone to strike that spot.

This I prove first: because either the air moves at an unequal rate with the earth; or it moves equally rapidly. If not equally, then it is certain the stone could not land at that spot, since the earth's movement would outstrip the stone borne by the air. If equally rapidly, then again the stone could not land at that spot, since although the air was moving in itself at an equal speed, yet on that account it could not carry the stone thus rapidly with itself and carrying it downward falling by its own weight, for the stone tending by gravity towards the center resists the carrying of the air.

You will say: if the earth is moved in a circle, so are all its parts; wherefore that stone in falling not only moves in a circle by the carrying of the air, but also in a circle because of its own nature as being part of the earth and having the same motion with it.

Verily this answer is worthless. For although the stone is turned in a circle by its own nature like the earth, yet its own natural gravity impeded it so that it is borne along that much the less swiftly, unlike the air or the earth, both of which are in their natural places and which in consequence have no gravity as a stone falling from on high has.

Lastly; because although the stone is moved in the world by its own nature like the whole earth, yet it is not borne along as swiftly as the whole earth. For as one stone by its own weight falls from the heaven following its own direct motion straight to the center just as a part of the earth, so also the whole earth itself would fall; and yet it would not fall so swiftly as the whole earth, for although the stone would be borne along in its sphere like the whole earth just as a part of it, yet it would not be borne along as swiftly as the whole earth; and so, in whatever way it is said, the motion of the earth ought always to outstrip the stone and leave it a long distance behind. Thus a stone could never fall at the point selected or a point perpendicularly beneath it. This is false. Ergo.

Ninthly: If the earth is moved in a circular orbit, it ought to pass from the west through the meridian to the east; consequently the air ought to move by the same path. But if this were so, then if an archer shot toward the east, his arrow ought to fly much farther than if he shot toward the west. For when he shot toward the east, the arrow would fly with the natural movement of the air and would have that supporting it. But when he shot toward the west, he would have the motion of the air against him and then the arrow would struggle against it. But it is certain the arrow ought to go much farther and faster when the movement of the air is favorable to it then when against it, as is obvious in darts sent out with a favoring wind. Ergo.

Similarly not a few other arguments can be worked out, but there are none as valuable for proof as the foregoing ones. Though these were written by me with a flying pen far from books and sick in bed with a broken leg, yet they seem to me to have so much value that I do not see any way by which they could rightly be refuted. These I have written for your gracious lordships in gratitude for your goodwill on the occasion of our conversation at your dinner four days ago; and I ask for them that you meditate on them justly and well.

# BIBLIOGRAPHY
## (of references cited.)

### I
### General Works.

Addis and Arnold: *Catholic Dictionary*, 2nd edit. London, 1884.

Bailly: *Histoire de l'Astronomie Moderne depuis la Fondation de l'Ecole d'Alexandrie, jusqu' a l'Epoque de 1730*. 3 vol. Paris, 1785.

Berry, Arthur: *Short History of Astronomy*. New York, 1912.

Cajori, Florian: *The Teaching and History of Mathematics in the United States*. Washington, 1890. (Bureau of Education, No. 3.)

Delambre, J.B.J.: *Histoire de l'Astronomie Ancienne*. Paris, 1817.

— —: *Histoire de l'Astronomie du Moyen Age*. Paris, 1819.

— —: *Histoire de l'Astronomie Moderne*. Paris, 1821.

De Morgan, Augustus: *A Book of Paradoxes*. 2 vol. 2nd edit. ed. by David Eugene Smith. Chicago, 1915.

Di Bruno, Joseph Faà: *Catholic Belief, or a short and simple exposition of Catholic Doctrine*. Author's American edit. 375th thousand. New York, [1912.]

Jacoby, Harold: *Astronomy, a Popular Handbook*. New York, 1913.

Janssen, J.: *History of the German People at the Close of the Middle Ages*. Trans. by Mitchell and Christie. 2 vol. St. Louis, no date.

Lecky, Wm. E. Hartpole: *History of England in the 18th Century*. 8 vol. New edit. New York, 1892.

Libri, C.: *Histoire des Sciences Mathématiques en Italie depuis la Renaissance des Lettres*. 2me édit. 4 vol. Halle, 1865.

Milman, Henry H.: *History of Latin Christianity*. 8 vol. in 4. New York, 1899.

Owen, John: *The Skeptics of the Italian Renaissance*. 2nd edit. New York, 1893.

Peignot, G.: *Dictionnaire Critique Littéraire et Bibliographique des Principaux Livres Condamnés au Feu, Supprimés on Censurés.* 2 vol. Paris, 1806.

Putnam, George Haven: *The Censorship of the Church of Rome.* 2 vol. New York, 1907.

Rashdall, Hastings: *Universities of Europe in the Middle Ages.* 2 vol. Oxford, 1895.

Smith, David Eugene: *Rara Arithmetica.* Boston, 1908.

Snyder, Carl: *The World Machine: The Cosmic Mechanism.* London, 1907.

Stephen, Leslie: *History of English Thought in the 18th Century.* 2 vol. 3rd edit. New York, 1902.

Taylor, Henry Osborne: *The Mediæval Mind.* 2nd edit. London, 1914.

Walsh, J.J.: *Catholic Churchmen in Science.* 2nd series. Philadelphia, 1909.

— —: *The Popes and Science.* Knights of Columbus edit. New York, 1911.

Wegg-Prosser, F.R.: *Galileo and his Judges.* London. 1889.

Whewell, William: *History of the Inductive Sciences from the Earliest to the Present Time.* New edit. revised. 3 vol. London, 1847.

White, Andrew D.: *History of the Welfare of Science with Theology in Christendom.* 2 vol. New York, 1898.

Windle, B.C.A.: *A Century of Scientific Thought and Other Essays.* London, 1915.

Young, Charles: *Manual of Astronomy.* Boston, 1902.

## II

### Special Works.

Allaben, Frank: *John Watts de Peyster.* 2 vol. New York, 1908.

— —: see De Peyster.

Anon: *Galileo – The Roman Inquisition: A Defence of the Catholic Church from the Charge of having persecuted Galileo for his philosophical opinions.* Reprinted from the *Dublin Review* with an introduction by an "American Catholic." Cincinnati, 1844.

Baudrillart, Henri: *Jean Bodin et son Temps: Tableau des Théories Politiques et des Idées Economiques au 16me siècle.* Paris, 1853.

Bartholmèss, Christian: *Jordano Bruno.* 2 vol. Paris, 1846.

Berti, Domenico: *Vita di Giordano Bruno da Nola.* Turin, 1868.

Bertrand, M.J.: *Copernic et ses Travaux* (Fév. 1864) in *Mémoires sur les Mathématiques.*

— —: *Le Procès de Galilée* (Oct. 1877), in *Eloges Académiques, nouvelle série*. Paris, 1902.

— —: *Notice sur la Vie et les Travaux de Kepler*. (Dec. 1863) in *Mémoires de l'Académie des Sciences*, XXXV. Paris, 1866.

Betten, Francis S. (S.J.): *The Roman Index of Forbidden Books briefly explained for Catholic Booklovers and Students*. 4th edit. enlarged. St. Louis, 1915.

Beyersdorf, Robert: *Giordano Bruno und Shakespeare*. Leipsic, 1889.

Blavatsky, H.P.: *The Secret Doctrine*. 2 vol. Point Loma, Cal., 1909.

Brewster, David: *Martyrs of Science: Lives of Galileo, Tycho Brahe and Kepler*. London, 1874.

Bridges, J.H.: *Tycho Brahe*, in *Contemp. Rev.*: 81: 196-213 (Feb. 1902).

Brinton, Daniel G. and Davidson, Thomas: *Giordano Bruno, Philosopher and Martyr*. Philadelphia, 1890.

Burckhardt, F.: *Zur Erinnerungaan Tycho Brahe. Vortrag 23, Oct. 1901, in den Naturforschen der Gesellschaft in Basel*. Vol. 13, Basel, 1901.

Chasles, Philarète: *Galilei, sa vie, son procès et ses contemporains*. Paris, 1862.

Conway, Bertrand L. (C.S.P.): *The Condemnation of Galileo*. Pamphlet. New York, 1913.

Cumont, Franz: *Astrology and Religion among the Greeks and Romans*. New York, 1912.

Davidson: see Brinton.

De l'Epinois, Henri: *Galilée, son procès, sa condemnation, d'après des documents inédits*, in *Revue des Quest. Hist.*, III, 68-145. Paris, 1867.

Desdouits, Théophile: *La Légende Tragique de Jordano Bruno*. Paris, 1885.

Dreyer, J.L.E.: *Tycho Brahe: A Picture of Scientific Life and Work in the 16th Century*. Edinburgh, 1890.

Eastman, Charles R.: *Earliest Predecessors of Copernicus*, in *Pop. Sci.* LVIII: 323-327 (April, 1906).

Fahie, J.J.: *Galileo, his Life and Work*. London, 1903.

Flammarion, Camille: *Vie de Copernic et Histoire de la Découverte du Système du Monde*. Paris, 1872.

Frisch: *Vita Joannis Kepler* in *Opera Omnia Kepleri*. VIII, 668-1028.

Frith, I.: *Life of Giordano Bruno the Nolan*. London, 1887.

Graux, Charles: *L'Université de Salamanque* in *Notices Bibliographiques*. Paris, 1884.

Haldane, Elizabeth S.: *Descartes, his Life and Times*. London, 1905.

Heath, Thomas L.: *Aristarchus of Samos, the Ancient Copernicus*. Oxford, 1913.

Holden, E.S.: *Copernicus* in *Pop. Sci.* LXV: 109-131 (June, 1904.)

La Fuente, (Vicente de): *Historia de las Universidades ... de España*. 2 vol. 1884.

Martin, Henri T.: *Galilée, les Droits de la Science et la Méthode des Sciences Physiques*. Paris, 1868.

McIntyre, J. Lewis: *Giordano Bruno*. London, 1903.

Monchamp, Georges: *Galilée et la Belgique, Essai Historique sur les Vicissitudes du Système du Copernic en Belgique*. Saint-Trond, 1892.

Parchappe, Max: *Galilée, sa Vie, ses Découvertes et ses Travaux*. Paris, 1866.

Prowe, Leopold: *Nicolaus Coppernicus*, 3 vol.: I and II, Biography, 1883; III, Sources, 1884. Berlin.

R — —: *Beitrage zur Beantwortung der Frage nach der Nationalität des Nicolaus Copernicus*. Pamphlet. Breslau, 1872.

Reusch, F.H.: *Der Process Galilei's und Die Jesuiten*. Bonn, 1879.

Robinson, James Howard: *The Great Comet of 1680: A Study in the History of Rationalism*. Northfield, Minn., 1916.

Schiaparelli, G.V.: *Die Vorlaufer des Copernicus im Alterthum*, trans. by M. Curtze. Leipsic, 1876.

— —: *Studj Cosmologici: Opinioni e Ricerche degli Antichi sulle Distance e sulle Grandezze dei Corpi Celesti*. Pamphlet. 1865.

Schwilgué, Charles: *Description Abregée de l'Horloge Astronomique de la Cathédrale de Strasbourg*, 6me édit. Strasbourg, 1856.

Shields, Charles W.: *The Final Philosophy*. New York, 1877.

Small, Robert: *Account of the Astronomical Discoveries of Kepler, — including an historical review of the Systems which had successively prevailed before his time*. London, 1804.

Thayer, William Roscoe: *Throne-Makers*. New York, 1899. -308: Giordano Bruno: his Trial, Opinions and Death.

Walsh, J.J.: *An Early Allusion to Accurate Methods in Diagnosis*. Pamphlet. 1909.

Warren, William F.: *The Earliest Cosmologies*. New York, 1909.

Vaughan, Roger Bede: *Life and Labours of S. Thomas of Aquin*. 2 vol. London, 1871.

Von Gebler, Karl: *Galileo Galilei and the Roman Curia*, trans. by Mrs. Sturge. London, 1879.

Ziegler, Alexander: *Regiomontanus, ein geistiger Vorlaufer des Columbus.* Dresden. 1874.

## III
### Sources.

*A: Pre-Copernican (chapters I and II).*

Archimedes: *Arenarius,* vol. II in *Opera Omnia* ed. Heiberg, Leipsic, 1781.

Aquinas, Thomas: *Summa Theologica,* vol. V in *Opera Omnia ... cum commentariis ... Caietani....* Rome, 1889.

Aristotle: *De Mundo,* vol. III in *Opera Omnia.* Paris, 1854.

Augustine: *De Civitate Dei,* vol. XLI in Migne: *Patr. Lat.* (Cf. trans. in vol. II in Nicene and Post-Nicene Christian Library. New York, 1903.)

— —: *De Genesi,* vol. XXXIV in Migne: *Pair. Lat.*

Bacon, Roger: *Opus Tertium,* vol. I in *Opera Quædam Hactenus Inedita,* ed. by Brewer. London, 1859.

Capella, Martianus: *De Nuptiis Philologiæ et Mercurii et de Septem Artibus Liberalibus, libri novem.* Ed. by Kopp. Frankfort, 1836.

Cicero: *Academica,* ed. by J.S. Reid, London, 1885. (Cf. trans. by Yonge in Bohn Classical Library, London, 1902.)

Clement of Alexander: *Stromatum,* vol. III in *Opera Omnia,* Leipsic, 1834 (Cf. trans. by Williams, vol. II in *Writings,* Edinburgh, 1869.)

Cusanus, Nicolaus: *De Docta Ignorantia,* and *Sermones,* in *Opera.* Basle, [1565.]

Diogenes Laërtius: *De Clarorum Philosophorum Vitis,* ed. Cobet. Paris, 1878. (Cf. trans. by Yonge in Bohn Classical Library, London, 1909.)

St. Dionysius the Areopagite: *De Cælesti Ierarchia,* vol. CXXII in Migne: *Patr. Lat.*

St. Isidore: *De Ordine Creaturarum,* vol. LXXXIII in Migne: *Patr. Lat.*

Lactantius: *Divinarum Institutionum,* vol. VI in Migne: *Patr. Lat.* (Cf. trans. by Fletcher, vol. XXI in Ante-Nicene Christian Library, Edinburgh, 1871.)

Lombard, Peter: *Sententiæ,* vol. CXCII in Migne: *Patr. Lat.*

Origen: *De Principiis,* vol. XI in Migne: *Patr. Græc.* (Cf. trans. vol. X in Ante-Nicene Christian Library, Edinburgh, 1869.)

St. Philastrius: *De Hæeresibus,* vol. XII in Migne: *Patr. Lat.*

Philo Judæus: *De Mundi Creatione* (vol. I), and *Quis Rerum Divinarum Hæres* (vol. IV) in *Opera Omnia,* Erlangæ, 1820. (Cf. trans. by Yonge, London, 1854.)

Plato: *Timæus*, vol. IV in *Opera* ed. Burnet, Oxford, [1905.] (Cf. trans. by Jowett, vol. III of *Dialogues*, 3rd edit. revised. New York, 1892).

Plutarch: *Moralia*, ed. Bernardakis, Teubner, Leipsic, 1893. (Cf. trans. ed. by Goodwin, Boston, 1898.)

Ptolemy, Claudius: *Syntaxis Mathematica*, vol. I in *Opera Quæ Supersunt Omnia*, 3 vol., Teubner, Leipsic, 1898. (Cf. trans. into French by Halma, 2 vol., Paris, 1813.)

Sacro Bosco: *Libellus de Sphæra*, Venice, 1488; Wittenberg, [1537]; Wittenberg, 1545; Paris, 1564; Venice, 1574; Wittenberg, 1578.

Scotus, Joannus: *Depositiones super Ierarchias sancti Dionysii*, vol. CXXII in Migne: *Patr. Lat.*

Seneca: *Naturalium Quæstionum Libros VIII*, ed. Gercke, vol. II in *Opera quæ supersunt*, Teubner, Leipsic, 1907. (Cf. trans. by Clarke, London, 1910.)

Vitruvius: *De Architectura Libri Decem*, Teubner, Leipsic, 1867. (Cf. trans. by Gwilt, London, 1880.)

*B: Copernican and Post-Copernican.*

Addison, Joseph: *The Spectator, No. 420*, vol. IV in *Works*. New edit. with notes. 6 vol. London, 1811.

Agricola, Georgius Ludovicus: *De Systemate Mundi Copernico, Disputatio Astronomica*. Pamphlet. Wittenberg, 1665.

Allaben, see Schoepffer.

"Anglo-American": *Copernicus Refuted: or the True Solar System*. Pamphlet. Baltimore, 1846.

Bacon, Francis: *Philosophical Works*. Reprinted from texts and translations of Ellis and Spedding, ed. by Robertson. London, 1905.

Barocio, Francisco: *Cosmographia in quatuor libros*. Venice, 1585.

Bayle, Pierre: *Système Abregé de Philosophie*, vol. III in *Oeuvres Diverses*. 4 vol. The Hague, 1731.

Bodin, Jean: *Universæ Naturæ Theatrum in quo rerum omnium effectrices causa et fines contemplantur et continuæ series quinque libris discutiuntur*. Frankfort, 1597.

— —: *Universæ Naturæ Theatrum*, trans. into French by François de Fougerolles. Lyons, 1597.

Boscovich, Rogerio Josepho (S.J.): *De Determinanda Orbita Planetæ ope catoptricæ*. Rome, 1749.

— —: *Opera Pertinentia ad Opticam et Astronomiam*. 5 vol. Bassan, 1785.

Bottrigaro, Hercole: *Trattato della Descrittone della Sfera Celeste in Piano di Cl. Tolomeo Tradotto in parlare Italiano*. Bologna, 1572.

Brahe, Tychonis: *Opera Omnia, sive Astronomiæ Instauratæ Progymnasmata*. Frankfort, 1648.

Browne, Thomas: *Pseudodoxia Epidemica* in *Works*, ed. by S. Wilkins. 3 vol. London, 1852.

Bruno, Giordano: *De Immenso et Innumerabilis*, in *Opera Latina Conscripta*, ed. by Fiorentino. Naples, 1884.

— —: *La Cena de le Ceneri*, in *Opere Italiane*, ed. by Gentile. Bari, 1907.

Burnet, Thomas: *The Sacred Theory of the Earth*. 5th Edit., 2 vol. London, 1722.

Burton, Richard: *Anatomy of Melancholy*. 13th edit. corrected, 2 vol. London, 1827.

Calvin, Jean: *Commentaria* in *Opera Omnia* in *Corpus Reformatorum*, vol. LIX. Brunswick, 1887.

— —: *Traité ou Avertissement contre l'Astrologie qu'on appelle Judiciaire et autre curiosités qui regnent aujourd'hui au monde*, in *Oeuvres François*, ed. by P.L. Jacob. Paris, 1842.

Canevari, Petro, Giovannelli, Andrea, Giovannelli, Benedicto: *De Observationibus Astronomicis. Dissertatio habita in Seminario Romano*. Rome, 1742.

Cassini, G.D.: *De l'Origine et du Progrès de l'Astronomie et de son usage dans la Géographie et dans la Navigation*, in *Recueil d'Observations faites en plusieurs voyages par ordre de sa majesté pour perfectionner l'Astronomie et la Géographie, par MM. de l'Académie Royale des Sciences*. Paris, 1693.

Cavalieri, Bonaventura: *Sfera Astronomica, Lettore primario delle Matematiche nello studio di Bologna ... cavate da MS. dell'Autore da Antonio Manari*. Rome, 1690.

Copernicus, Nicolas: *De Revolutionibus Orbium Cœlestium, Libri sex*. Nürnberg, 1543.

— —: *Astronomia Instaurata, Libris sex comprehensa, qui De Revolutionibus Orbium Cœlestium, inscribuntur. Nunc demum post 75 ab obitu authoris annum integritati suæ restituta, notisque illustrata, opera et studio Nicolai Mulerii*. Amsterdam, 1617.

— —: *De Revolutionibus Orbium Cœlestium. Libri Sex. Accedit G.J. Rhetici Narratio Prima, cum Copernici nonnullis Scriptis minoribus nunc primum collectis, ejusque vita*. (In Latin and Polish). Warsaw, 1854.

— —: *De Revolutionibus Orbium Cœlestium, Libri Sex*, with Rheticus, George Joachim: *Narratio Prima*. Thorn, 1873.

— —: see also vol. III, Sources, of Prowe: *Nicolaus Coppernicus.*

Cromer, Martin: *De Origine et Rebus Gestibus Polonorum Libri XXX. Tertium ab authore diligenter recogniti.* Basel, 1568.

— —: *Poloniæ*, in *Res Publicæ sive Status Regni Poloniæ, Lituanæ, Prussiæ, Livoniæ, etc. Diversorum Autorum.* Lugd: Batavorum, 1642.

DuBartas, W. deSaluste: *The Divine Weeks*, trans. by Josuah Sylvester, (1501) ed. by T.W. Haight. Waukesha, Wis. 1908.

De Brisbar, J.: *Calendrier Historique ... avec un Traité Historique de la Sphère.* 2me édit. Leyden, 1697.

De Maupertius: *Eléments de Géographie*, in *Ouvrages Divers*. Amsterdam, 1744.

De Premontval, Mme.: *Le Méchaniste Philosophe, Mémoir ... de la Vie et des Ouvrages du Sr. Jean Piegeon, mathématicien, Membre de la Société des arts, Auteur des premières Sphères mouvantes qui ayent été faites en France, selon l'hypothèse de Copernic.* The Hague, 1750.

DePeyster, J.W., Allaben, F.: *Algol: The "Ghoul" or "Demon" Star, a Supplement to "The Earth Stands Fast."* Pamphlet. New York, 1900.

Descartes, Réné: *Les Principes de la Philosophie*, vol. III in *Oeuvres* ed. by Cousin. II vol. Paris, 1824.

Di Gallo, Marco Antonio Giovanni Gianesimi: *Opinione sopra il movimento della Terra e degli Astri.* Pamphlet. Bassano, 1771.

Dobell, John (ed.): *Hymns.* No title-page. Preface dated England, 1806.

Favaro, Antonio: *Galileo e l'Inquisizione, Documenti de Processo Galileiano ... per la prima volta integralmente pubblicati.* Florence, 1907.

Fénelon, F. de S. de la Mothe: *Traité de l'existence et des attributs de Dieu*, in vol. I, *Oeuvres*. 3 vol. Paris, 1835.

Ferramosca, Aegidius Leognanus: *Positiones suas Physioastronomicas De Sphæra Cœlesti publice Demonstrandas et Propugnandis in Collegio Neapolitano Soc. Jesu.* Naples, 1682.

Fienus, Thomas, Fromundus, Liberti: *De Cometa Anni 1618, Dissertationes. Ejusdem Thomæ Fieni Epistolica quæstio, An Verum sit Cœlum moveri, et Terram quiescere?* London, 1655. Bound with Fromundus: *Meteorologicorum.*

Fienus, Thomas: *Epistolica quæstio.* See above.

Fontana, Cajetano: *Institutio Physico-Astronomica.* Mutinæ, 1695.

Forbes, Duncan: *A Letter to a Bishop concerning some important Discoveries in Philosophy and Theology*, in *Works*. Dublin, 1755.

Foscarini, Paolo Antonio: *An Epistle Concerning the Pythagorian and Copernican Opinion of the Mobility of the Earth and Stability of the Sun ... in which* the Authorities of Sacred Scriptures ... are reconciled. Written to the Most Reverend Father Sebastiano Fontoni, General of the Order of Carmelites, Jan., 1615, Naples, in Salusbury: Math. Coll., q.v.

Fromondus, Liberti: Ant-Aristarchus sive Orbis-Terræ Immobilis: Liber Unicus in quo decretum S. Congregationis S.R.E. Cardinal, an 1616 adversus Pythagorico-Copernicanos editum defenditur. Antwerp, 1631.

——: Meteorologicorum Libri Sex. Cui accessit in hac ultima Editione Thomæ Fieni et Lib. Fromondi Dissertationes de Cometa Anni 1618, et Clarorum Virorum Judicia De Pluvia Purpurea Bruxelliensis. London, 1656.

——: Vesta, sive Ant-Aristarchi vindex adversus Iac. Lansbergium ... in quo Decretum ... 1616 et alterum anno adversus Copernicanos terræ motores editum, iterum defenditur. Antwerp, 1634. See also Fienus.

Gadbury, John and Timothy: George Hartgill's Astronomical Tables. London, 1656.

Galilei, Galileo: Opere, Edizione Nazionale, ed. by Favaro. 20 vol. Florence, 1890-1909.

——: Dialogo sopra i due Massimi sistemi del Monde, Tolemaico, e Copernicano. Florence, 1632. Trans. in Salusbury: Math. Coll., q.v.

——: Lettera a Madama Cristina di Lorena, Granduchessa di Toscana, in vol. V, Opere; trans. in Salusbury: Math. Coll., q.v.

——: Sidereus Nuncius ... atque Medicea Sidera, in vol. III, Opere.

Accusation, Condemnation and Abjuration of Galileo Galilei before the Holy Inquisition at Rome, 1633. Pamphlet. London, 1819. See also Favaro.

Gassendi, Petro: Institutio Astronomica juxta Hypothesis quam Veterum quam Copernici ac Tychonis. 3rd edit. Hagæ-Comitum, 1656.

——: Institutio Astronomica.... 5th edit. London, 1675.

——: Institutio Astronomica juxta Hypothesis Tam Veterum quam Recentiorum Cui accesserunt Galileo Galilei; Nuncius Sidereus, et Johannis Kepleri: Dioptrice. 3rd edit. corrected. London, 1683.

——: Vita Tychonis Brahei, Equitis Dani, Astrononum Coryphæi., 2nd edit. corrected. Hagæ-Comitum, 1655.

George, Earl of Macclesfield: Speech in the House of Peers, Mar. 18, 1750. Pamphlet. London, 1751.

Gilbert, William: De Magnete, Magnetis qui corporibus, et de magno magnete tellure Physilogia nova. London, 1600, reprinted Berlin 1892. Trans. by P.F. Mottelay, New York, 1893.

Herbert, George: Man, in English Works ed. by G.H. Palmer, Boston, 1905.

Horne, George: *Commentary on Book of Psalms*. 2 vol. Oxford, 1784.

— —: *A Fair, Candid and Impartial State of the Case between Sir Isaac Newton and Mr. Hutchinson*. Pamphlet. Oxford, 1753.

Hutchinson, John: *Moses's Principia*. London, 1724.

Huygens, Christian: *The Celestial Worlds discover'd. Trans. from the Latin*. London, 1698.

— —: *Nouveau Traité de la Pluralité des Mondes ... traduit du Latin en François par M.D.* Amsterdam, 1718.

*Index Librorum Prohibitorum ... usque 1681*, (appendix to June, 1704). Rome, 1704.

— — *usque 1711*. Rome, 1711.

— — *usque 1744*. Rome, 1744.

— — *usque 1752*. Rome, 1752.

— — *Benedicti XIV*. Rome, 1758.

— — *Pii Sexti*. Rome, 1786.

— — *Pii Septimi*. Rome, 1819.

— — *editum 1835*. Mechlin, 1838.

— — *Gregorii XVI*. Rome, 1841.

— — *Leonis XIII recognitus Pii X*. 3rd edit. Rome, 1911.

Justus-Lipsius: *Physiologiæ Stoicorum*, vol. IV, in *Opera Omnia*, 4 vols. Vesaliæ, 1674.

Keble, John: *Christian Year*. Ed. by Lock. London, 1895.

Keill, John: *Introductio ad Veram Astronomiam, seu Lectiones Astronomicæ habitæ in Schola Astronomica Academiæ Oxoniensis*. Oxford, 1718.

Kepler, Joannis: *Opera Omnia*, edidit Frisch. 8 vol. Frankfort a.M. 1858-1871.

— —: *Abstract of the "Introduction Upon Mars"*, trans. in Salusbury: *Math. Coll.*, q.v.

— —: *Tabulæ Rudolphinæ ... a Phœnice illo Astronomorum Tychone ... primum concepta ... 1564 ... observatioribus siderum ... post annum præcipue 1572 ... Traducta in Germaniam ... 1598. Tabulas ipsas ... jussu et stipendiis ... Imp. Rudolphi*. Ulm, 1627.

Kircher, Athanasius (S.J.): *Iter Exstaticum Cœleste*, enlarged by Gaspare Schotto, S.J. Herbipoli, 1671.

Kromer, see Cromer.

La Galla, Julius Cæsar: *De Phænomenis in Orbe Lunæ Novi Telescopii usu a Gallileo Gallileo. Physica Disputatio.* Venice, 1612.

Lambert: *Système du Monde.* 2me édit. Berlin, 1784.

Lange, J.R.L.: *The Copernican System: The Greatest Absurdity in the History of Human Thought.* No place, 1901.

Leadbetter, Charles: *Astronomy of the Satellites of the Earth, Jupiter and Saturn, grounded upon Sir Isaac Newton's Theory of the Earth's Satellites.* London, 1729.

Longomontanus, Christianus: *Astronomica Danica.* Amsterdam, 1640.

Luther, Martin: *Tischreden oder Colloquia*, ed. by Forstemann. 4 vol. Leipsic, 1846.

Mather, Cotton: *The Christian Philosopher, a Collection of the Best Discoveries in Nature with Religious Improvements.* London, 1721.

Melancthon, Philip: *Initia Doctrinæ Physicæ*, 2nd edit. Wittenberg, 1585.

Milton, John: *Areopagitica*, ed. by Hales. Oxford, 1904.

— —: *Paradise Lost*, in *Complete Poetical Works*, ed. by Beeching. London, 1911.

Montaigne, Michel E. de: *Apologie of Raymond Sebonde*, vol. II in *Essayes*, trans. by Florio. 3 vol. London, 1908.

Moxon, Joseph: *A Tutor to Astronomie and Geographie, or an Easie and Speedy Way to know the use of both the Globes, Celestial and Terrestrial.* 2nd edit. London, 1670.

Mulerius, Nicolaus: *Tabulæ Friscæ Lunæ-Solares quadruplices è fontibus Cl. Ptolemæi, Regis Alfonsi, Nic. Copernici et Tychonis Brahe.* Amsterdam, 1611.

Piccioli, Gregorio: *La Scienza dei Cieli e dei Corpi Celesti, e loro meravigliosa Posizione, Moto, e Grandezza: Epilogata colle sue Figure quattro più famosi Sistemi dell'Universo Tolemaico, Copernicano, Ticonico, e Novissimo. Colla patente Dimostrazione della quieta di nostra Terra, e che poco più, o meno ci apparisce ella oggidi nella sua superfizie tal quale era avanti l'Universal Diluvio.* Verona, 1741.

Pike, Samuel: *Philosophica Sacra: or the Principles of Natural Philosophy extracted from Divine Revelation.* London, 1753.

Pluche: *Histoire du Ciel considéré selon les idées des Poêtes, des Philosophes et de Moïse.* 2 vol. Paris, 1739.

Pope, Alexander: *Letter* in vol. VI, *Works*, new edit. by Croker and Elwin. London, 1871.

Record, Robert: *The Castle of Knowledge*. 3rd edit. London, 1596.

Reisch, Gregorius: *Margarita Filosofica...* trans. into Italian by Gallucci. Venice, 1599.

Rheticus, Georgius Joachim: *De Libris Revolutionum ad Joannem Schönerum Narratio Prima*, 1539, in Copernicus: *De Revolutionibus*, Thorn, 1873.

Riccioli, Giovanni Baptista (S.J.): *Almagestum Novum, Astronomiam veterem novamque completens Observationibus Aliorum et Propriis, Novisque Theorematibus, Problematibus ac Tabulis promotam.* 2 vol. Bologna, 1651.

— —: *Apologia pro Argumento Physicomathematico contra Systema Copernicanum adiecto contra illud Novo Argumento ex Reflexo motu Gravium Decidentium.* Venice, 1669.

Spooner, W.W.: *Great Copernican Myth*; a Review of Algol by de Peyster and Allaben. Pamphlet. Tivoli, N.Y., 1901.

Salusbury, Thomas: *Mathematical Collections and Translations, first tome.* London, 1661.

Schoepffer, C.: *The Earth Stands Fast*, trans. for and ed. by J.W. de Peyster with notes and Supplement by Frank Allaben. Pamphlet. New York, 1900.

Schotto, Gaspar (S.J.): *Organum Mathematicum. Opus Posthumum,* Herbipoli, 1668.

Simpson, Thomas: *Essays on Several Curious and Useful Subjects in Speculative and Mix'd Mathematicks.* London, 1740.

Sindico, Pierre: *Refutation du Système de Copernic exposé en dix-sept lettres qui été adressées à feu M. Le Verrier.* Paris, 1878.

Spagnio, Andrea: *De Motu.* Rome, 1774.

Tischner, August: *Le Système Solaire se Mouvant.* Pamphlet. Leipsic, 1894.

Toland, John: *Miscellaneous Works.* 2 vol. London, 1747.

Vitali, Hieronymo: *Lexicon Mathematicum.* Rome, 1690.

Voight, Johann-Henrich: *Der Kunstgünstigen Einfalt Mathematischer Raritäten Erstes Hundert: Allen Kunstgünstigen zum lustigen und nutzbaren Gebrauch mit Fleiss und Mühe zusammen geordnet und furgetragen.* Hamburg, 1668.

Wesley, John: *Sermon*, vol. VII in *Works*. 5th edit. 14 vol. London, 1860.

— —: *Survey of the Wisdom of God in the Creation, or a Compendium of Natural Philosophy.* 3 vol. in 2. 2nd edit. Bristol, 1770.

Whiston, William: *A New Theory of the Earth.* 4th edit. London, 1725.

Wilkins, G.: *The First Book: The Discovery of a New World.* 3rd edit. London, 1640.

— —: *The Second Book: Discourse concerning a New Planet, that 'tis probable our Earth is one of the planets.* London, 1640. (Bound with *First Book.*)

"W.R.": *The New Astronomer, or Astronomy made easy by such instruments that readily shew by Observation the Stars....* London, 1735.

# INDEX

Johnson, S.,
Justus-Lipsius,
Keble, J.,
Keill, J.,
Kepler,
Knap,
Kromer, M.,
Lactantius,
Lalande,
Lange, J.R.,
Lansberg,
Leo X,
Liège, Univ. of,
Longomontanus,
Louvain, Univ. of,
Luther,
Lutherans,
Mæstlin,
Martianus Capella,
Mather, Cotton,
Melancthon,
Milton,
Mivart,
Montaigne,
*Narratio Prima*,
Newton,
Nicolas Cusanus,
Origen,
Osiander,
Owen, J.,
Paul III,
Paul V,
Peter Lombard,
Peter the Great,
Philastrius,
Philo Judæus,
Philolaus,
Piegeon, J.,
Pike, S.,
Pius VII,
Plato,
Plutarch,

Pope, Alexander,
Pseudo-Dionysius,
Ptolemy,
theory,
Pürbach,
Pythagoras,
Pythagoreans,
Recorde, R.,
Regiomontanus,
Reinhold, Erasmus,
Rheticus,
Riccioli,
Roberts,
Roemer,
Sacrobosco,
Salamanca, Univ. of,
Schoepffer, C.,
Schwilgué,
Settele,
Shakespeare,
Sindico,
Stephen, Leslie,
Thomas Aquinas,
Turrettin,
Turrinus, J.,
Tycho Brahe,
theory,
Urban VIII,
Van Welden, M.,
Vitruvius,
Voight, J.H.,
von Schönberg, N.,
Wallis,
Wesley, J.,
Whewell,
Widmanstadt,
Wilkins, Bp.,
Wren, Dean,
Yale, Univ. of,
Zytphen,

# FOOTNOTES

[1] The earliest observation Ptolemy uses is an Egyptian one of an eclipse occurring March 21, 721 B.C. (Cumont: 7). [In these references, the Roman numerals refer to the volume, the Arabic to the page, except as stated otherwise. The full title is given in the bibliography at the back under the author's name.]

[2] Warren: 40. See "Calendar" in Hastings: *Ency. of Religion and Ethics*.

[3] For a summary of recent researches, see the preface of Heath: *Aristarchus of Samos*. For further details, see Heath: *Op. cit.*, and the writings of Kugler and Schiaparelli.

[4] See Plutarch: *Moralia: De placitas Philosophorum*, Lib. I et II, (V. 264-277, 296-316).

[5] Diogenes Laërtius: *De Vitis*, Lib. IX, c. 3 (252).

[6] Plato: *Timæus*, sec. 39 (III, 459 in Jowett's translation).

[7] Aristotle: *De Mundo*, c. 2 et 6 (III, 628 and 636).

[8] Plutarch: *Op. cit.*, Lib. III, c. 2 (V, 303-4).

[9] Diogenes Laërtius: *De Vitis*, Lib. VIII, c. 1, et 8 (205, 225).

[10] Diogenes: *Op. cit.*, Lib. VIII, c. 7 (225).

[11] Cicero: *Academica*, Lib. II, c. 39 (322).

[12] Plutarch: *Op. cit.*, Lib. II (V. 299-300).

[13] Archimedes: *Arenarius*, c. 1. Delambre: *Astr. Anc.*, I, 102.

[14] This is the only account of his system. Even the age in which he flourished is so little known that there have been many disputes whether he was the original inventor of this system or followed some other. He was probably a contemporary of Cleanthes the Stoic in the 3rd century B.C. He is mentioned also by Ptolemy, Diogenes Laërtius and Vitruvius. (Schiaparelli: *Die Vorlaufer des Copernicus im Alterthum*, 75. See also Heath: *Op. cit.*)

[15] Plutarch: *Op. cit.*: Bk. III, c. 2 (V, 317-318).

[16] The Stoic contemporary of Aristarchus, author of the famous Stoic hymn. See Diogenes Laërtius: *De Vitis*.

[17] Plutarch: *De Facie in Orbe Lunæ*, (V, 410).

[18] Young: 109.

[19] Milton: *Paradise Lost*, Bk. VIII, ll. 82-85.

[20] Vitruvius: *De Architectura*, Lib. IX, c. 4 (220).

[21] Martianus Capella: *De Nuptiis*, Lib. VIII, (668).

[22] Ptolemy: *Almagest*, Lib. I, c. 7, (1, 21-25). Translated in Appendix B.

[23] Whewell: I, 239.

[24] Whewell: I, 294.

[25] Berry: 79.

[26] His book *De Motu Stellarum*, translated into Latin by Plato Tiburtinus (fl. 1116) was published at Nuremberg (1557) by Melancthon with annotations by Regiomontanus. *Ency. Brit.* 11th. Edit.

[27] Vaughan: I, 281.

[28] Graux: 318.

[29] Graux: 319.

[30] Rashdall: II, pt. I, 77.

[31] *Dict. of Nat. Biog.*

[32] MSS. of it are extremely numerous. It was the second astronomical book to be printed, the first edition appearing at Ferrara in 1472. 65 editions appeared before 1647. It was translated into Italian, French, German, and Spanish, and had many commentators. *Dict. of Nat. Biog.*

[33] Whewell: I, 277.

[34] Blavatski: II, 29, note.

[35] Philo Judæus: *Quis Rerum Divinarum Hæres.* (IV, 7).

[36] Clement of Alexandria: *Stromatum*, Lib. V, c. 14, (III, 67).

[37] Origen: *De Principiis*, Lib. I, c. 7, (XI, 171).

[38] Lactantius: *Divinarum Institutionum*, Lib. III, c. 3 (VI, 355).

[39] Ibid: Lib. III, c. 24, (VI, 425-428).

[40] Taylor: *Mediæval Mind*, I, 74.

[41] By the will of God the earth remains motionless and stands throughout the age.

[42] Augustine: *De Civitate Dei*, Lib. XVI, c. 9, (41).

[43] Augustine: *De Genesi*, II, c. 9, (v. 34). (White's translation).

[44] Augustine: *Civitate Dei*, Lib. V, c. 5, (v. 41).

[45] Philastrius: *De Hæresibus*, c. 133, (v. 12).

[46] Pseudo-Dionysius: *De Cœlesti Ierarchia*, (v. 122).

[47] Milman: VIII,-9. See the *Paradiso*.

[48] Isidore of Seville: *De Ordine Creaturarum*, c. 5, sec. 3, (v. 83).

[49] Lombard: *Sententia*, Bk. II, Dist. I, sec. 8, (v. 192).

[50] Aquinas: *Summa Theologica*, pt. I, qu. 70, art. 2. (*Op. Om. Caietani*, V, 179).

[51] Roger Bacon: *Opus Tertium*, 295, 30-31.

[52] Ibid: 289.

[53] Ibid: 282.

[54] Delambre: *Moyen Age*, 365.

[55] Prowe: II, 67-70.

[56] Delambre: *Moyen Age*, 262-272.

[57] Delambre: *Moyen Age*, 272.

[58] It has been claimed that Regiomontanus knew of the earth's motion around the sun a hundred years before Copernicus; but a German writer has definitely disproved this claim by tracing it to its source in Schöner's *Opusculum Geographicum* (1553) which states only that he believed in the earth's axial rotation. Ziegler: 62.

[59] Ibid: 62.

[60] Delambre: *Op. cit.*: 365.

[61] Janssen: *Hist. of Ger.*, I, 5.

[62] *Cath. Ency.*: "Cusanus."

[63] From Cues near Treves.

[64] Cusanus: *De Docta Ignorantia*, Bk. II, c. 11-12: "Centrum igitur mundi, coincideret cum circumferentiam, nam si centrum haberet et circumferentiam, et sic intra se haberet suum initium et finem et esset ad aliquid aliud ipse mundus terminatus, et extra mundum esset aluid et locus, quæ omnia veritate carent. Cum igitur non sit possibile, mundum claudi intra centrum corporale et circumferentiam, non intelligitur mundus, cuius centrum et circumferentia sunt Deus: et cum hic non sit mundus infinitus, tamen non potest concipi finitus, cum terminis careat, intra quos claudatur. Terra igitur, quæ centrum esse nequit, motu omni carere non potest, nam eam moveri taliter etiam necesse est, quod per infinitum minus moveri posset. Sicut igitur terra non est centram mundi.... Unde licet terra quasi stella sit, propinquior polo centrali, tamen movetur, et non describit minimum circulum in motu, ut est ostensum.... Terræ igitur figura est mobilis et sphærica et eius motus circularis, sed perfectior esse posset. Et

quia maximum in perfectionibus motibus, et figuris in mundo non est, ut ex iam dictis patent: tunc non est verum quod terra ista sit vilissima et infima, nam quamvis videatur centralior, quo'ad mundum, est tamen etiam, eadem ratione polo propinquior, ut est dictum." (-39).

[65] Riccioli: *Alm. Nov.*, II, 292.

[66] Cusanus: *Opera*, 549: Excitationum, Lib. VII, ex sermone: *Debitores sumus*: "Est enim oratio, omnibus creaturis potentior. Nam angeli seu intelligentiæ, movent orbes, Solem et stellas: sed oratio potentior, quia impedit motum, sicut oratio Josuæ, fecit sistere Solem."

[67] Di Bruno: 284, 286a; Walsh: *An Early Allusion*, 2-3.

[68] *Nicolaus Coppernicus* (Berlin, 1883-4; 3 vol.; Pt. I, Biography, Pt. II, Sources), by Dr. Leopold Prowe gives an exhaustive account of all the known details in regard to Copernicus collected from earlier biographers and tested most painstakingly by the documentary evidence Dr. Prowe and his fellow-workers unearthed during a lifetime devoted to this subject. (*Allgemeine Deutsche Biographie*.) The manuscript authority Dr. Prowe cites (Prowe: I, 19-27 and footnotes), requires the double p in Copernicus's name, as Copernicus himself invariably used the two p's in the Latinized form *Coppernic* without the termination *us*, and usually when this termination was added. Also official records and the letters from his friends usually give the double p; though the name is found in many variants — Koppernig, Copperinck, etc. His signatures in his books, his name in the letter he published in 1509, and the Latin form of it used by his friends all bear testimony to his use of the double p. But custom has for so many centuries sanctioned the simpler spelling, that it seems unwise not to conform in this instance to the time-honored usage.

[69] Prowe: I, 85.

[70] *Ency. Brit.*: "Thorn."

[71] Prowe: I, 47-53.

[72] These facts would seem to justify the Poles today in claiming Copernicus as their fellow-countryman by right of his father's nationality and that of his native city. Dr. Prowe, however, claims him as a "Prussian" both because of his long residence in the Prussian-Polish bishopric of Ermeland, and because of Copernicus's own reference to Prussia as "unser lieber Vaterland." (Prowe: II, 197.)

[73] Prowe: I, 73-82.

[74] Ibid: I, 111.

[75] Ibid: I, 124-129.

[76] Ibid: I, 137.

[77] Ibid: I, 141-143.

[78] Rheticus: *Narratio Prima*, 448 (Thorn edit.).

[79] Prowe: I, 154.

[80] Ibid: I, 169.

[81] Ibid: I, 174.

[82] Ibid: I, 175. This insured him an annual income which amounted to a sum equalling about $2250 today. Later he received a sinecure appointment besides at Breslau. (Holden in *Pop. Sci.*, 111.)

[83] Prowe: I, 224.

[84] Ibid: I, 308.

[85] Ibid: I, 240 and note. Little is known about him today, except that he was primarily an observer, and was highly esteemed by his immediate successors; see Gilbert: *De Magnete*.

[86] Clerke in *Ency. Brit.*, "Novara."

[87] Prowe: I, 249.

[88] Prowe: I, 279.

[89] Ibid, 294.

[90] Ibid: I, 319.

[91] Prowe: I, 335-380.

[92] Ibid: II, 75-110, 116, 124.

[93] Ibid: II, 204-8.

[94] Ibid: II, 110.

[95] Ibid: II, 144.

[96] Ibid: II, 146.

[97] Ibid: II, 293-319.

[98] Ibid: II, 464-472.

[99] Ibid: II, 170-187.

[100] Holden in *Pop. Sci.*, 109.

[101] Prowe: II, 67-70.

[102] Copernicus: *De Revolutionibus*, Thorn edit., 444. The last two words of the full title: *De Revolutionibus Orbium Cœlestium* are not on the original MS. and are believed to have been added by Osiander. Prowe: II, 541, note.

[103] Ibid: II, 490-1.

[104] Copernicus: Dedication, 4. (Thorn edit.)

[105] Prowe: II, 503-508.

[106] Ibid: II, 64.

[107] Ibid: II, 58-9.

[108] Rheticus: *Narratio Prima*.

[109] Prowe: II, 56.

[110] Copernicus: Dedication, 5-6. See Appendix B.

[111] For a translation of this dedication in full, see Appendix B. In the original MS. occurs a reference (struck out) to Aristarchus of Samos as holding the theory of the earth's motion. (Prowe: II, 507, note.) The finding of this passage proves that Copernicus had at least heard of Aristarchus, but his apparent indifference is the more strange since an account of his teaching occurs in the same book of Plutarch from which Copernicus learned about Philolaus. But the chief source of our knowledge about Aristarchus is through Archimedes, and the editio princeps of his works did not appear till 1544, a year after the death of Copernicus. C.R. Eastman in *Pop. Sci.* 68:325.

[112] Delambre: *Astr. Mod.* pp. xi-xii.

[113] As the earth moves, the position in the heavens of a fixed star seen from the earth should differ slightly from its position observed six months later when the earth is on the opposite side of its orbit. The distance to the fixed stars is so vast, however, that this final proof of the earth's motion was not attained till 1838 when Bessel (1784-1846) observed stellar parallax from Königsberg. Berry: 123-24.

[114] *Commentariolus* in Prowe: III, 202.

[115] Holden in *Pop. Sci.*, 117.

[116] Delambre: *Astr. Mod.*, p. xi.

[117] Snyder: 165.

[118] Copernicus: Dedication, 3.

[119] Prowe: II, 362-7.

[120] Ibid: II, 406.

[121] Ibid: II, 501.

[122] Ibid: II, 517-20.

[123] Four other editions have since appeared; at Basel, 1566, Amsterdam 1617, Warsaw 1847, and Thorn 1873. For further details, see Prowe: II, 543-7, and Thorn edition pp. xii-xx. The edition cited in this study is the Thorn one of 1873.

[124] Prowe: II, 553-4.

[125] Copernicus: *De Revolutionibus*, I. "To the reader on the hypotheses of this book."

[126] "For it is not necessary that these hypotheses be true, nor even probable, but this alone is sufficient, if they show reasoning fitting the observations."

[127] Kepler: *Apologia Tychonis contra Ursum* in *Op. Om.*: I, 244-246.

[128] Prowe: II, 251, note.

[129] Ibid: II, 537-9.

[130] Ibid: II, 273.

[131] Ibid: II, 286-7.

[132] A second copy was found at Upsala shortly afterwards, though for centuries its existence was unknown save for two slight references to such a book, one by Gemma Frisius, the other by Tycho Brahe. Prowe: II, 284.

[133] Ibid: II, 273-4.

[134] Prowe: II, 274, note.

[135] Prowe: II, 426-440.

[136] Ibid: II, 387-405.

[137] Ibid: II, 391.

[138] Holden in *Pop. Sci.*, 119.

[139] Prowe: II, 233-244.

[140] Burckhardt: 8.

[141] The two standard lives of Tycho Brahe are the *Vita Tychonis Brahei* by Gassendi (1655) till recently the sole source of information, and Dreyer's *Tycho Brahe* (1890) based not only on Gassendi but on the documentary evidence disclosed by the researches of the 19th century. For Tycho's works I have used the *Opera Omnia* published at Frankfort in 1648. The Danish Royal Scientific Society has issued a reprint (1901) of the rare 1573 edition of the *De Nova Stella*.

[142] Bridges: 206.

[143] Dreyer: 11-84.

[144] Gassendi: 2.

[145] Dreyer: 13.

[146] Gassendi: 9-10.

[147] Dreyer: 38-44.

[148] Ibid: 84.

[149] Ibid: 234-5.

[150] Kepler: *Tabulæ Rudolphinæ*.

[151] Dreyer: 317-363.

[152] As stated in his Book on the Comet of 1577 (pub. 1588).

[153] Dreyer: 168-9.

[154] Schiaparelli in Snyder: 165.

[155] Brahe: *Op. Om.*, pt. I,.

[156] Ibid: 409-410.

[157] The Tychonic system has supporters to this day. See chap. v.

[158] Dreyer: 181.

[159] The authoritative biography is the *Vita* by Frisch in vol. VIII, -1028 of *Op. Om. Kep.*

[160] Frisch: VIII, 718.

[161] Delambre: *Astr. Mod.* 314-315.

[162] Frisch: VIII, 999.

[163] Ibid: VIII, 696.

[164] Ibid: VIII, 699-715.

[165] Dreyer: 290-309.

[166] Frisch: VIII, 715.

[167] Bertrand:-1.

[168] The two laws first appeared in 1609 in his *Physica Cœlestis tradita commentarius de motu stellæ martis*. (Frisch: VIII, 964.) The third he enunciated in his *Harmonia Mundi*, 1619. (Ibid: VIII, 1013-1017.)

[169] "Cor et animam meam": Kepler's expression in regard to the Copernician theory. Ibid: VIII, 957.

[170] Ibid: VIII, 838.

[171] Ibid: VIII, 742.

[172] Kepler: *Op. Om.*, I, 106: *Præfatio ad Lectorem*.

[173] Berry: 210.

[174] Berry: 265.

[175] Ibid: 359.

[176] Jacoby: 89.

[177] See before.

[178] Luther: *Tischreden*, IV, 575; "Der Narr will die ganze Kunst Astronomiæ umkehren. Aber wie die heilige Schrift anzeigt, so heiss Josua die Sonne still stehen, und nicht das Erdreich."

[179] "Non est autem hominis bene instituti dissentire a consensu tot sæculorum." Præfatio Philippi Melanthonis, 1531, in Sacro-Busto: *Libellus de Sphæra* (no date).

[180] "Vidi dialogum et fui dissuassor editionis. Fabula per sese paulatim consilescet; sed quidam putant esse egregiam *katorthoma* rem tam absurdam ornare, sicut ille Sarmaticus Astronomis qui movet terram et figet solem. Profecto sapientes gubernatores deberent ingeniorum petulantia cohercere." *Epistola B. Mithobio*, 16 Oct. 1541. P. Melancthon: *Opera*: IV, 679.

[181] "Quamquam autem rident aliqui Physicum testimonia divina citantem, tamen nos honestum esse censemus, Philosophiam conferre ad cœlestia dicta, et in tanta caligine humanæ mentis autoritatem divinam consulere ubicunque possumus." Melancthon: *Initia Doctrinæ Physicæ*: Bk. I, 63.

[182] Ibid: 60.

[183] Ibid: 59-67.

[184] Farrar: *Hist. of Interpretation*: Preface, xviii: "Who," asks Calvin, "will venture to place the authority of Copernicus above that of the Holy Spirit?"

[185] Calvin: *Oeuvres François: Traité ... contre l'Astrologie*, 110-112.

[186] Calvin: *Op. Om.* in *Corpus Reformatorum*: vol. 25, 499-500; vol. 59, 195-196.

[187] "Ce planétaire ... represente le système du monde tel qu'il a été expliqué par Copernic."

[188] Schwilgué:.

[189] Ibid:.

[190] *Dict. of Nat. Biog.*: "Recorde."

[191] Quoted , from the edition of 1596 in the library of Mr. George A. Plimpton. See also Recorde's *Whetstone of Witte* (1557) as cited by Berry, 127.

[192] DuBartas: *The Divine Weeks* (Sylvester's trans. edited by Haight): Preface, pp. xx-xxiii and note.

[193] *Op. cit.*: 72.

[194] La Fuente: *Historia de la Universidades ... de España*: II, 314.

[195] *Doc. 86* in Favaro: 130.

[196] *Diccionario Enciclopédico Hispano-Americano de literatura, ciencias y artes* (Barcelona, 1898).

[197] Quoted in Salusbury: *Math. Coll.*: I, 468-470 (1661), as a work inaccessible to most readers at that time because of its extreme rarity. It remained on the Index until the edition of 1835.

[198] Montaigne: *Essays*: Bk. II, c. 2: *An Apologie of Raymonde Sebonde* (II, 352).

[199] This book, published at Frankfort in 1597, was translated into French by M. Fougerolles and printed in Lyons that same year. It has become extremely rare since its "atheistic atmosphere" (Peignot: *Dictionnaire*) caused the Roman Church to place it upon the Index by decree of 1628, where it has remained to this day.

[200] Cromer in History of Poland.

[201] Cromer in History of Poland.[A]

[A] I could not find this reference in either of Martin Kromer's books; *De Origine et Rebus Gestis Polonorum, ad 1511*, or in his *Res Publicæ sive Status Regni Poloniæ*.

[202] Bodin: *Univ. Nat. Theatrum*: Bk. V, sec. 2 (end).

[203] Delambre: *Astr. Mod.*: I, 663.

[204] Justus-Lipsius: *Physiologiæ Stoicorum*: Bk. II, dissert. 19 (Dedication 1604, Louvain), (IV, 947); "Vides deliria, quomodo aliter appellent?"

[205] Berti: 285.

[206] McIntyre: 3-15.

[207] Four lives of Bruno have been written within the last seventy-five years. The first is *Jordano Bruno* by Christian Bartholmèss (2 vol., Paris 1846). The next, *Vita di Giordano Bruno da Nola* by Domenico Berti (1868, Turin), quotes in full the official documents of his trial. Frith's *Life of Giordano Bruno* (London, 1887), has been rendered out of date by J.L. McIntyre's *Giordano Bruno* (London, 1903), which includes a critical bibliography. In addition, W.R. Thayer's *Throne Makers* (New York, 1899), gives translations of Bruno's confessions to the Venetian Inquisition. Bruno's Latin works (*Opera Latina Conscripta*), have been republished by Fiorentino (3 vol., Naples, 1879), and the *Opere Italiane* by Gentile (3 vol., Naples, 1907).

[208] Bartholmèss: I, 134.

[209] Libri: IV, 144.

[210] McIntyre: 16-40.

[211] Bartholmèss: I, 134.

[212] Gilbert: *De Magnete* (London, 1600).

[213] Berti: 369, Doc. XIII.

[214] McIntyre: 16-40.

[215] Bartholmèss: I, 134.

[216] Beyersdorf: *Giordano Bruno und Shakespear*, 8-36.

[217] Such passages as *Troilus and Cressida*: Act I, sc. 3; *King John*, Act III, sc. 1; and *Merry Wives*, Act III, sc. 2, indicate that Shakespeare accepted fully the Ptolemaic conception of a central, immovable earth. See also Beyersdorf: *op. cit.*

[218] McIntyre: 68.

[219] Ibid: 47-72.

[220] See official documents in Berti: 327-395.

[221] Bruno: *De Immenso et Innumerabilis*: Lib. III, cap. 9 (vol. 1, pt. 1, 380-386).

[222] Thayer: 268.

[223] Berti: 285.

[224] Ibid: 282.

[225] Fahie: 82-89.

[226] Thayer: 299.

[227] The publication of A. Favaro's *Galileo e l'Inquisizione: Documenti del Processo Galileiano ... per la prima volta integralmente pubblicati*, (Firenze, 1907), together with that of the National Edition (in 20 vols.) of Galileo's works, edited by Favaro (Firenze, completed 1909), renders somewhat obsolete all earlier lives of Galileo. The more valuable, however, of these books are: Martin's *Galilée* (Paris, 1868), a scholarly Catholic study containing valuable bibliographical notes; Anon. (Mrs. Olney): *Private Life of Galileo*, based largely on his correspondence with his daughter from which many extracts are given; and von Gebler's *Galileo Galilei and the Roman Curia* (trans. by Mrs. Sturge, London, 1879), which includes in the appendix the various decrees in the original. Fahie's *Life of Galileo* (London, 1903), is based on Favaro's researches and is reliable. The documents of the trial have been published in part by de l'Epinois, von Gebler and Berti, but Favaro's is the complete and authoritative edition.

[228] Fahie: 20-40.

[229] Ibid: 121.

[230] Galileo: *Opere*, X, 68.

[231] 'The Second Day' in Salusbury: *Math. Coll.* I, 110-111.

[232] Fahie: 265.

[233] Conway: 46-47.

[234] Conway: 46-47.

[235] Fahie: 77-126.

[236] Doc. in Favaro: 13.

[237] Fahie: 149.

[238] Galileo: *Opere*, V, 281-288.

[239] Doc. in Favaro: 48-49.

[240] Doc. in Favaro: 49.

[241] Ibid: 38: "amorevole avviso."

[242] Ibid: 46, 47, 51.

[243] Ibid: 47.

[244] Ibid: 49.

[245] Ibid: 43-45, see original in Galileo: *Opere*, V, 281-285.

[246] Doc. in Favaro: 78.

[247] Ibid: 61.

[248] Ibid: 61.

[249] Doc. in Favaro: 61-62.

[250] Ibid: 88.

[251] Ibid: 80-86.

[252] Ibid: 145.

[253] Ibid: 16.

[254] Doc. in Favaro: 16.

[255] Monchamp: 46.

[256] Fromundus: *De Cometa Anni* 1618: chap. VII,. (From the private library of Dr. E.E. Slosson. A rare book which Lecky could not find. *History of Rationalism in Europe*, I, 280, note.)

[257] In 1620 the Congregation issued the changes it required to have made in the *De Revolutionibus*. They are nine in all, and consist mainly in changing assertion of the earth's movement to hypothetical statement and in striking out a reference to the earth as a planet. Doc. in Favaro: 140-141. See illustration.

[258] Doc. in Favaro: 149.

[259] Galileo: *Dialogo*: To the Reader.

[260] Doc. in Favaro: 70.

[261] Fahie: 230.

[262] Ibid: 240.

[263] Doc. in Favaro: 88-89.

[264] Ibid: 66.

[265] Ibid: 17-18.

[266] Galileo: *Opere*, XV, 26.

[267] Doc. in Favaro: 74.

[268] Ibid: 75.

[269] Ibid: 76.

[270] Ibid: 80-81.

[271] Ibid: 80-81.

[272] Doc. in Favaro: 83.

[273] Ibid: 84.

[274] Ibid: 85-87.

[275] Ibid: 101.

[276] Doc. in Favaro: 101.

[277] Doc. in Favaro: 146.

[278] Ibid: 145.

[279] Ibid: 103, 129.

[280] Ibid: 134.

[281] Milton: *Areopagitica*: 35.

[282] Doc. in Favaro: 135.

[283] Ibid: 137.

[284] Fahie: 402.

[285] Doc. in Favaro: 138; and Fahie: 402.

[286] Doc. in Favaro: 101, 103.

[287] Ibid: 104-132.

[288] Fahie: 325, note.

[289] For full statement, see Martin: 133-207.

[290] Gebler: 263.

[291] See Gebler: 244-247; White: I, 159-167; also Martin.

[292] Martin: 136; and Salusbury: *Math. Coll.* "To the reader."

[293] Galileo: *Opere*, XV, 25.

[294] Putnam: I, 310.

[295] De Morgan: I, 98.

[296] Martin: 140.

[297] *Cath. Ency.*: "Boscovich."

[298] Doc. in Favaro: 159.

[299] Ibid: 30, 31.

[300] In Salusbury: *Math. Coll.*: I, 471-503.

[301] Bk. II: sec. 8, §1.

[302] Bk. II, ch. 46.

[303] *Phil. Works*: 705.

[304] Bk. III.

[305] *Phil. Works*: 684-685.

[306] Translated in Appendix C. For criticism, see Monchamp: 58-64.

[307] Fromundus: *Vesta*: Ad Lectorem.

[308] Monchamp: 41.

[309] Justus-Lipsius: IV, 947.

[310] Monchamp: 48.

[311] Ibid: 94.

[312] Galileo: *Opere*: XV, 25.

[313] Ibid: XIV, 340-341.

[314] Monchamp: 107-108.

[315] Doc. in Favaro: 120-121, 132, 133.

[316] Monchamp: 125, 143.

[317] Ibid: 148-149.

[318] Ibid: 152-153.

[319] Ibid: 182-234.

[320] Monchamp: 321.

[321] Agricola: *Disputatio*.

[322] Schotto: *Organum Mathematicum* (1667).

[323] Voight: *Der Kunstgünstigen Einfalt Mathematischer Raritäten Erstes Hundert*. (Hamburg, 1667).

[324] Voight: *op. cit.*: 28.

[325] Ibid: 30-31.

[326] Longomontanus: *Op. cit.*: 162.

[327] Longomontanus: *Op. cit.*: 158.

[328] Riccioli: *Alm. Nov.*: Præfatio, I, xviii.

[329] Riccioli: *Alm. Nov.*: II, 496.

[330] *Cath. Ency.*: "Riccioli," and Walsh: Catholic Churchmen in Science: 200. (2nd series, 1909.)

[331] Riccioli: *Alm. Nov.*: II, 288-289; see frontispiece.

[332] Riccioli: *Alm. Nov.*: II, 288-289; see frontispiece.

[333] Delambre: *Astr. Mod.*: I, 674-680.

[334] Riccioli: *Apologia*: 2.

[335] Riccioli: *Alm. Nov.*: II, 313, 315.

[336] Riccioli: *Alm. Nov.*: II, 330-351.

[337] Ibid: II, 339-340.

[338] Delambre: *Op. cit.*: I, 677.

[339] Ibid: I, 673.

[340] Riccioli: *Alm. Nov.*: II, 290.

[341] Riccioli: *Op. cit.*: II, 304, 309.

[342] Delambre: *Astr. Mod.*: I, 680.

[343] Riccioli: *Op. cit.*: II, 478 (condensed), 500.

[344] Riccioli: *Apologia*: 4.

[345] Ibid: 103.

[346] One bit of contemporary opinion on Riccioli and his work has come down to us. A canon at Liège, René-François Sluse, wrote asking a friend (about 1670) to sound Wallis, the English mathematician, as to his opinion of the *Almagestum Novum*, and of this argument based on the acceleration of movement in falling bodies. Wallis himself replied that he thought the argument devoid of all value. The canon at once wrote, "I do not understand how a man as intelligent as Riccioli should think he could bring to a close a matter so difficult [the refutation] by a proof as futile as this." Monchamp: 165-166.

For a full, annotated list of books published against the Copernican system between 1631-1688, see Martin: *Galilée*: 386-388.

[347] See Moxon: *Advice, A Tutor to Astronomy and Geography* (1670): 269.

[348] Haldane's *Descartes* (1905) is the most recent and authoritative account based upon Descartes's works as published in the Adams-Tannery edition (Paris, 1896. foll.). This edition supersedes that of Cousin.

[349] Haldane: 153.

[350] Ibid: 158.

[351] Descartes: *Principes*, Pt. III, chap. 13.

[352] Haldane: 291.

[353] Monchamp: 185, note.

[354] Haldane: 292.

[355] Ibid: 193, 279.

[356] Monchamp: 177-181.

[357] Berry quotes a passage from Thomas Digges (d. 1595) with the date 1590: "But in this our age, one rare witte (seeing the continuall errors that from time to time more and more continually have been discovered, besides the infinite absurdities in their Theoricks, which they have been forced to admit that would not confess any mobility in the ball of the Earth) hath by long studye, paynfull practise, and rare invention delivered a new Theorick or Model of the World, shewing that the Earth resteth not in the Center of the whole world or globe of elements, which encircled or enclosed in the Moone's orbit, and together with the whole globe of mortality is carried round about the Sunne, which like a king in the middst of all, rayneth and giveth laws of motion to all the rest, sphærically dispersing his glorious beames of light through all this sacred celestiall Temple." Browne also refers to Digges (I, 383).

[358] Gilbert: *De Magnete*, Bk. VI, c. 3-5 (214-228).

[359] Johnson: *Life*, in Browne: I, xvii.

[360] Browne: I, 35.

[361] Burton: *Anatomy of Melancholy*, I, 1; I, 66. First edition, 1621; reprinted 1624, 1628, 1632, 1638, 1651-2, 1660, 1676.

[362] Ibid: I, 385, 389.

[363] Herbert: II, 315.

[364] Milton: *Paradise Lost*, Bk. VIII, lines 159 *et seq.*
The great Puritan divine, John Owen (1616-1683), accepts the miracle of the sun's standing still without a word of reference to the new astronomy. (*Works*: II, 160.) Farrar states that Owen declared Newton's discoveries were against the evident testimonies of Scripture (Farrar: *History of Interpretation*: xviii.), but I have been unable to verify this statement. Owen died before the *Principia* was published in 1687.

[365] Whewell: I, 410.

[366] Wilkins: *Discourse Concerning a New Planet.*

[367] Salusbury: *Math. Coll.*: To the Reader.

[368] Whewell: I, 411.

[369] One London bookseller in 1670 advertised for sale "spheres according to the Ptolmean, Tychonean and Copernican systems with books for their use." (Moxon: 272.) In 1683 in London appeared the third edition of Gassendi's *Institutio*, the textbook of astronomy in the universities during this period of uncertainty. It too wavers between the Tychonic and the Copernican systems.

[370] *Dict. of Nat. Biog.*: "Keill."

[371] Keill: *Introductio ad Veram Astronomiam.*

[372] Cajori: 29-30.

[373] Cajori: 37.

[374] Pope: *Works*, VI, 110.

[375] Addison: *Spectator*, No. 420, (IV, 372-373). An interesting contrast to this passage and a good illustration of how the traditional phraseology continued in poetry is found in Addison's famous hymn, written a year later:

"Whilst all the stars that round her [earth] burn
And all the planets in their turn,
Confirm the tidings as they roll,
And spread the truth from pole to pole.

"What though in solemn silence all
Move round this dark terrestrial ball;
What though no real voice nor sound
Amidst their radiant orbs be found;

"In reason's ear they all rejoice,
And utter forth a glorious voice;
Forever singing, as they shine,
'The hand that made us is divine'."

[376] Mather: *Christian Philosopher*, 75, 76.

[377] Leadbetter: *Astronomy* (1729).

[378] In de Maupertius: *Ouvrages Divers*, (at the back).

[379] Wesley: *Compendium of Natural Philosophy*, I, 14, 139.

[380] Dobell: *Hymns*, No. 5, No. 10.

[381] Keble: *Christian Year*, 279.

[382] Horne: *Fair, Candid, Impartial Statement ...*, 4.

[383] Pike: *Philosophia Sacra*, 43.

[384] Forbes: *Letter*, (1755).

[385] See Wesley: I, 136-7.

[386] *Dict. of Nat. Biog.*: "Hutchinson."

[387] Stephen: *Hist. of Eng. Thought*: I, 390.

[388] Ibid: 391.

[389] de Premontval: *Le Méchaniste Philosophe*, 54, 72. (The Hague, 1750).

[390] de Brisbar: *Calendrier Historique*, (Leyden), 228-233.

[391] Bayle: *Système Abregé de Philosophie* (The Hague, 1731), IV, 394-412.

[392] de Maupertius: *Eléments de Géographie*, xv, 9-14.

[393] de Premontval: 123.

[394] Ibid: 132.

[395] Ibid: 157.

[396] Cassini: *De l'Origine et du Progrès ...*, 35.

[397] Shields: 59. I have failed to find this reference in Bossuet's works.

[398] Fénelon: *Oeuvres*, I, 3 and 7.

[399] Pluche: *Histoire du Ciel*: viii, ix, xiii.

[400] *Cath. Ency.*: "Boscovich."

[401] *Opera*: III (1785).

[402] Cited in Monchamp: 335 note.

[403] Ibid: 326.

[404] Ibid: 330.

[405] Fontana: *Institutio*, II, 32-35.

[406] Ferramosca: *Positiones ...*: 19.

[407] Piccoli: *La Scienza*, 4, 7.

[408] Spagnio, *De Motu*, 81.

[409] Monchamp: 331.

[410] Monchamp: 345.

[411] Bailly: II, 132, note.

[412] Flammarion: 196-198.

[413] Shields: 60.

[414] White: I, 159-167.

[415] See di Bruno: *Catholic Belief*, 286a.

[416] Riccioli: *Apologia*, 103.

[417] White: I, 165. See the answer by Wegg-Prosser: *Galileo and his Judges*.

[418] Donat: 183.

[419] Walsh: *Popes and Science*, 17.

[420] Conway: 48.

[421] Anon.: *Galileo — the Roman Congregation*, 39, 60.

[422] De Morgan: I, 172.

[423] "Anglo-American": 5-6.

# ABOUT THE AUTHOR

Dorothy Stimson was an American scholar who lived from October 10, 1890, to September 19, 1988. From 1921 to 1947, she was the head of Goucher College, and from 1947 until 1955, she taught history there. Between 1953 and 1957, Stimson was the head of the History of Science Society. Her research looked at how the Copernican theory was received. She also put together a book of papers by George Sarton, who is thought to be the person who started the study of the history of science. Henry Albert Stimson and Alice Wheaton had Stimson on October 10, 1890, in St. Louis, Missouri. She was the granddaughter of a former president of Dartmouth College, and she was related to Henry L. Stimson, who was the former secretary of war for the United States. In 1912, Stimson got his Bachelor of Arts from Vassar College. Later, she went to school at Columbia University and got a master's degree in 1913 and a doctorate in 1917. The Gradual Acceptance of the Copernican Theory of the Universe was the title of her dissertation. James Harvey Robinson told Stimson to look into this subject, so he did. From 1921 to 1947, Stimson was the dean of women at Goucher College. She was also a history teacher at Goucher for a long time.

[424] Ibid: 11.

[425] De Morgan: II, 335.

[426] White: I, 150.

[427] Schoepffer: *The Earth Stands Fast.*

[428] Ibid: Supplement by Allaben, 21, 74.

[429] Ibid: Note by J.W. de P., 74.

[430] De Peyster and Allaben: *Algol*, preface.

[431] Lange: *The Copernican System: The Greatest Absurdity in the History of Human Thought.*

[432] De Peyster and Allaben: *Algol*, 74.

[433] Sindico: *Refutation du Système de Copernic....*

[434] Tischner: *Le Système Solaire se Mouvant.* (1894).

[435] White: I, 151.

[436] See translated sections in Appendix C.

[437] Robinson: 107.

[438] Ibid: 119.

[439] See Prowe: *Nic. Cop.*: III, 128-137.

[440] *i.e.*, the 15,000 solar years in which all the heavenly bodies complete their circuits and return to their original positions.

[441] Plutarch: *Moralia: De Placitis Philosophorum*, Lib. III, c. 13 (V. 326).

[442] These two sentences the Congregations in 1620 ordered struck out, as part of their "corrections."

[443] As Rabbi David testified on the 19th Psalm [these footnotes are by Bodin].

[444] Job: 38.

[445] Proverbs.

[446] Metaphysics: II. c. 6, de Cœlo. I. c. 6.

[447] In his last chapter.

[448] Which is confirmed by Pico of Mirandola: Heptaplus: Bk. V.

[449] Enchiridion: cap. 43; Gen.: 2 and 18.

[450] On Psalm: Audite cœli.

[451] Summa: pt. 1, art. 3, ques. 70.

[452] Metaphy. XII.

[453] In his commentaries on Book XII of Metaph. where he gives the opinion of Calippus and Eudoxus.

[454] Ex. XVIII and following. Philo Judæus in the Allegories.

[455] Aristotle: Metaph. II and XII and de Cœlo I.

[456] Gen.: 1.

[457] Chap. 1 and 10. Exod.: 24.

[458] I Kings: 8. Deut.: 28.

[459] Psalm 146.

[460] According to Maymon: Perplexorum, III.

[461] Psalm 147.

[462] Psalm 148. Gen. 1 and 7.

[463] Also in Psalm 67 and 123.

[464] Psalm 92.

[465] Exod. 24. Ezek. 1, 10.

[466] Isa. 6.

[467] Isa. 6. Ezek. 1 and 10. Zach. 4. Exod. 24, 25.

[468] Maleficium quidam, *i.e.*, some evil-power. Job 5.

[469] Augustine against Faustus wrote that vanity is not produced from the dust, nor evil from the earth.

[470] Job 41 and 49. Isa. 54. Ezek. 31.

[471] Isa. 54.

[472] Isa. 45.

[473] Job 34.

[474] Feyens probably refers here to Francesco Patrizzi, who was an enemy of the peripatetics and a great supporter of platonism. He died in 1597 at Rome, where Clement VIII had conferred on him the chair of philosophy.

[475] Joshua X: 13-14.

[476] Ecclesiastes I: 4.